A CALL BACK INTO

THE SECRET PLACE

DISCOVER GOD'S

DESIRE FOR

INTIMACY WITH

YOU.

© 2019, 2026 Suzeey Tina
All rights reserved.

No part of this publication may be reproduced, stored in a retrieval system, or transmitted in any form or by any means—electronic, mechanical, photocopying, recording, or otherwise—without the prior written permission of the publisher, except for brief quotations in critical articles or reviews.

Scripture quotations are taken from the New King James Version of The Bible. Copyright ©1979, 1980, 1982. Thomas Nelson. Inc., Publishers

Used by permission. All rights reserved.

Published by Golden City Press [Johannesburg, South Africa]

ISBN:

Cover Design: Golden City Press
Interior Design and Layout: Golden City Press

Contact : goldencitypublishing@gmail.com

For more resources and updates, visit:
 facebook.com/Suzeeyannee

Printed in South Africa

Dedication

This book is dedicated to the glory of God and the advancement of His Kingdom. May every reader be drawn deeper into the heart of the Father through these words.

To my sons, David and Daniel, who will carry this message even to their generation.

Contents

A CALL BACK INTO THE SECRET PLACE	2
CHAPTER 1 HE TOLD ME..	8
CHAPTER 2 ADAM, WHERE ARE YOU?	15
CHAPTER 3 FOUNDATIONS OF SPIRITUAL WARFARE.	26
CHAPTER 4 BUSY SERVING	42
CHAPTER 5 WHO DO MEN SAY I AM?	50
CHAPTER 6 WHY DIDN'T YOU COME TODAY?	59
CHAPTER 7 THE FIRST TIME I HEARD HIM	67
CHAPTER 8 TO KNOW HIM IS TO HAVE ETERNAL LIFE.	88
CHAPTER 9 BREAKING FREE FROM THE RELIGIOUS SPIRIT	96
CHAPTER 10 NO ONE SEES ME AND LIVES	109
CHAPTER 11 THE CALL TO INTIMACY	121
CHAPTER 12 THE HILL OF THE LORD	128
CHAPTER 13 OBEDIENCE — GOD'S LOVE LANGUAGE	143
CHAPTER 14 THE COST OF THE SECRET PLACE	153
CHAPTER 15 THE SECRET PLACE RECLAIMED	161

PREFACE

A CALL BACK INTO THE SECRET PLACE

There is a sacred place that Heaven still calls us to — a place where words fall silent and only hearts speak. It is the Secret Place. The chamber of communion. The garden of whispers between God and His beloved.

For many, life's noise has slowly drowned out that call. Yet, the Lord is still yearning for hearts that will return —not just to church buildings or religious activity, but back to intimacy with Him. This book is that call. A call back into the quiet. Back into His presence. Back into the place where we are known and transformed.

Thank you for choosing to embark on this journey with me. I have been guided by the inspiration of the Holy Spirit to this point, and I'm eager to share my experiences and insights with you—hoping to ignite within you a deeper longing to know the Lord Jesus Christ personally and intimately.

Allow me to provide a glimpse into my own spiritual journey, particularly a transformative period during my college years in Texas. There, I encountered a group of remarkable women whose kindness and wisdom left an indelible mark on me. Their discussions often revolved around moments when they felt the Holy Spirit's guidance—a concept that both intrigued and challenged me.

You see, up until then, my interactions with God had mainly occurred through dreams. I would literally force myself to sleep, hoping that in the night hours, God would answer my questions or prayers. While these encounters were precious, my heart longed for something more—a living, breathing relationship like the one these women described. I wanted to hear Him.

So, with a little courage and a lot of curiosity, I approached one of them, asking how I could attune myself to God's voice. Her response was beautifully simple: "Spend time with Him." Those words struck a deep chord within me and set me on a lifelong pursuit of intimacy with the Lord.

From that moment, my journey became one of discovery—learning not only from others but from the Lord Himself. I began to realize that the true transformation doesn't come merely from knowing about God, but from knowing Him. The wisdom we gather is powerful, but it is the application of that wisdom that unlocks real spiritual growth.

My hope is that what you read in these pages won't remain as words or information, but that it will draw you into your own personal revival. That it will stir your spirit to action—into stillness, prayer, and intimacy with God.

I remember the early struggles vividly—feeling overwhelmed by Scripture and unsure how to make sense of its depth. But as I sought the Holy Spirit, the same One who inspired every word of the Bible, the pages began to breathe. Through prayerful study, I started to discern the living voice of God speaking directly to me.

And then one day, it happened—I heard Him. Not through a dream, not through another person, but directly. That moment changed everything. It reminded me that God is not far. He is near, waiting patiently for those who will come close enough to listen.

So, dear reader, this is your invitation. Whether you are seeking your first encounter or yearning to rekindle a lost flame, know this: the Lord is waiting in the Secret Place. Not with condemnation, but with love—a love that calls you by name.

May this book serve as your gentle nudge back into His presence.
May it awaken the part of you that was always meant to walk with Him in the cool of the day.
And as you read, may the Holy Spirit whisper again to your soul:
"Come away, My beloved."

Prayer for You

Heavenly Father, we lift up our hearts to You in reverence and adoration. May Your name be exalted now and forevermore.

As our reader embarks on this journey, may Your words leap off the pages and into their hearts, transforming them from deep within. Let this be more than just a book— let it be a conduit for Your divine presence and revelation.

Holy Spirit, we invite Your presence to dwell within the reader, guiding them into the depths of Your truth. Open their eyes to see, their ears to hear, and their hearts to receive Your love in abundance.

Break down every barrier and stronghold that hinders intimacy with You, O Lord. Let religion give way to relationship, and may Your love reign supreme in their lives.

In the mighty name of Jesus, we declare these prayers answered, believing in Your faithfulness and grace.
Amen.

CHAPTER 1

HE TOLD ME..

Isn't it remarkable that the inspiration to write this book came to me during my personal quiet time with the Holy Spirit? And now, here I am, inviting you to join me in spending time with Him as well. When I first sensed His prompting to write, I was overcome with excitement, and I began this journey with fervor.

As I delved into the process, I realized that every experience I've had in my walk with God has led me to this moment—a moment I cherish deeply as I share with you what I've discovered. And as you read, I pray you treasure these insights as much as I do.

I specifically had you in mind, the one reading these words. If you've started reading, it's likely because you're seeking answers, eager to understand the secrets of the secret place. So, let's embark on this journey together, for I believe it will change us profoundly.

I invite you to set aside distractions, grab a cup of coffee, and join me as we reconnect with our first love. He beckons us to return, and I am honored to serve as the messenger delivering His love letter to you.

Now, perhaps you've never thought of the Holy Spirit as a person, and you may find it perplexing when I refer to Him as "Him." Or maybe the concept of the Trinity—God the Father, God the Son, and God the Holy Spirit—leaves you puzzled. In our limited understanding, we struggle to grasp how God can be One yet manifest in three distinct persons.

Yet, as we immerse ourselves in Scripture, inspired by the Holy Spirit Himself, we begin to comprehend that God accommodates Himself to us. He divides

Himself so that we, as mortal beings, can approach Him, commune with Him, and relate to Him. And while mentors, pastors, and other spiritual leaders play crucial roles in our lives, God desires a personal connection with each of us.

It's natural to question whether we're doing things right, but what matters most is that you're here, seeking to grow. This book is for those who genuinely desire to encounter the Lord, and rest assured, He will reveal Himself to you.

If you're seeking power or spiritual gifts without prioritizing your relationship with God, you're on the wrong path. Jesus admonishes us to seek God first, and everything else will follow, everything else includes the needs, the gifts, the spiritual power etc. Your relationship with God is the foundation upon which everything else in your life rests.

So, I urge you to approach this journey with an open heart and mind. Together, let's uncover the mysteries of the secret place and understand why it's essential. Remember, without Jesus, nothing can truly prosper. As we delve deeper into this book, may God open your eyes and ears to His truth.

Let's proceed, eager to hear what the Spirit is saying to His church.

When I first began my journey as a new believer, I was deeply moved by the intimacy I saw others share with God. I admired how they spoke of Him with such closeness — how they prayed, listened, and seemed to live in constant fellowship with His presence. Inside me grew a longing, a hunger that words could barely express. I remember praying through tears, asking, *"Lord, when will You speak to me too?"*

What I didn't realize then was that God had *always* been speaking. His voice had never been silent — I simply wasn't yet positioned to hear Him clearly. My heart was restless, my thoughts loud, and my focus scattered. I was seeking Him everywhere *outside* of myself, unaware that He was waiting patiently in the stillness *within*.

This, I believe, has become a kind of spiritual pandemic in our world today. We search high and low for encounters with God — in people, in places, in experiences — when all along, He dwells in the quiet chambers of our own hearts. His presence isn't found in the noise of striving but in the peace of surrender.

In those early days, I made it my discipline to read the Word daily, as every believer should. I would often pause to ask Jesus questions about what I was reading — not realizing that He was actually listening. And more than that, He was answering. I just didn't recognize His voice yet.

Over time, I began to notice a pattern: whenever I asked a question, an unexpected clarity or understanding would come — an insight that was beyond my natural reasoning. That's when I began to tell myself, *"I may be intelligent, but I am not as intelligent as the Holy Spirit. I may have wisdom, but not the kind that comes from Him."*

Still, I didn't grasp that those gentle whispers, those sudden illuminations, were God Himself communicating with me.

One morning, during my usual time of prayer and study, I sat quietly on the floor of my room with my

Bible and journal. The world outside was still asleep, and in that sacred silence, I began to write — line upon line, precept upon precept — as revelation flowed effortlessly. And then, in the midst of that stillness, I heard Him speak so clearly in my heart:

"A time will come when I will take you back to where I got you from."

I froze. Could this really be God? My first instinct was disbelief. I told myself I was imagining it — that it was just my mind echoing my own thoughts. Yet, deep down, something in me *knew*.

I wrote the words down anyway, though I wrestled with doubt. But I have since learned that when the Lord speaks, He doesn't need to repeat Himself. His Word is already established, carrying life and power from the very moment it is released.

That experience marked the beginning of my understanding of how God speaks — not always through thunder or fire, but often through quiet impressions, gentle nudges, and words that linger in the spirit long after the moment has passed.

CHAPTER 2

ADAM, WHERE ARE YOU?

In the book of Genesis, we encounter a poignant scene where Adam and Eve hide from the presence of the Lord in the Garden of Eden. This passage offers profound insights into our relationship with God and the consequences of sin.

And they heard the sound of the Lord God walking in the garden in the cool of the day, and Adam and his wife hid themselves from the presence of the Lord God among the trees of the garden. Then the Lord God called to Adam and said to him, "Where are you?" So he said, "I heard Your voice in the garden, and I was afraid because I was naked; and I hid myself." And He said, "Who told you that you were naked? Have you eaten from the tree of which I commanded you that you should not eat?" Then the man said, "The woman whom You gave to be with me, she gave me of the tree, and I ate." And the Lord God said to the woman, "What is this you have done?"The woman said, "The serpent deceived me, and I ate."

Genesis 3:8-13

The setting is familiar: the Lord walks in the garden in the cool of the day, a routine encounter that Adam and his wife once welcomed eagerly. Yet, on this occasion, they hide among the trees, consumed by shame and fear. When God calls out to Adam, "Where are you?" it's not a question born out of ignorance but one that pierces through the barriers of guilt and separation.

Adam's response—or rather, his attempt to conceal himself—reveals a fundamental misconception about God. The serpent's lie, subtly planted in the minds of humanity, suggests that God distances Himself from those who fall short of His standards. But nothing could be further from the truth.

From this passage, we glean that God desires intimacy with His creation. He seeks us out, not to condemn but to restore. Our sins may separate us from Him, but His love remains constant, beckoning us back into His embrace.

I've come to understand firsthand that God is not the distant, unapproachable figure our minds sometimes portray Him to be. He longs for communion with us, His beloved children, and His love surpasses any flaws or shortcomings we may perceive in ourselves. As you read these words, I pray that the Father would remove any false notions you hold about Him. May He reveal Himself as the loving Father who eagerly awaits your return to intimacy with Him. You are deeply cherished, and He yearns for you to recognize your worth in His eyes.

Consider the significance of Adam's creation. He was formed by the hand of God, a masterpiece crafted with care and intention. Yet, in Jesus Christ, we encounter a new creation—a second Adam, birthed from the womb of God Himself, through the graced virgin Mary.

This profound truth transforms our understanding of who we are in God's eyes. We are not merely created beings but beloved children, born of His heart and infused with His divine DNA. When we grasp the depth of His love for us, it changes everything.

Being born again is more than a mere concept—it's a spiritual reality that reshapes our identity. We are no longer bound by our past or our shortcomings. Instead, we carry within us the very essence of God's love, a love that empowers us to love others unconditionally.

Let me take a moment to talk about what it truly means to be born again. Sadly, many people who faithfully attend church still struggle to understand this vital truth. They may participate in religious activities, serve in ministries, and even know the Scriptures well —yet have never personally experienced the new birth that Jesus spoke of.

The conversation between Jesus Christ and Nicodemus, a respected Pharisee and religious teacher, is one of the most important dialogues in the Bible to help us grasp this mystery. Nicodemus came to Jesus at night, seeking understanding, and Jesus went straight to the heart of the matter:

> *"Jesus answered and said to him, 'Most assuredly, I say to you, unless one is born again, he cannot see the kingdom of God.'*
> *Nicodemus said to Him, 'How can a man be born when he is old? Can he enter a second time into his mother's womb and be born?'*
> — John 3:3–4 (NKJV)

Nicodemus was puzzled. To him, the idea of being "born again" sounded impossible—something physical rather than spiritual. But Jesus was revealing a divine truth: to see and enter the Kingdom of God, one must experience a spiritual rebirth, not a natural one.

This is not about joining a church or following religious customs; it is about an inner transformation—a change in living, thinking, and being—that only the Holy Spirit can bring.

This was a powerful question that Nicodemus asked, and rightly so. Truthfully speaking, it is a concept that sounds strange to the natural ear. Yet within this mystery lies the very foundation of salvation and eternal life.

Nicodemus and the Search for More

Nicodemus came to Jesus under the cover of night, searching for understanding. He was a man of high reputation—a teacher, a scholar, and a religious leader—yet something within him knew there was more. His knowledge of Scripture could not quiet the restlessness in his heart.

When he heard about the miracles and teachings of Jesus, something within him stirred. He was drawn to something divine—something beyond human reason and religious form. And in that quiet nighttime conversation, Jesus revealed one of the greatest mysteries of the Kingdom:

"Unless one is born of water and the Spirit, he cannot enter the kingdom of God."

These words were not poetic; they were revolutionary. Jesus was describing a rebirth that no human effort could produce. The Pharisees emphasized strict obedience to the Law, but Jesus was pointing to something deeper—a change of nature, not merely behavior.

Born of Water

"Born of water" speaks of cleansing and repentance. Before the Spirit of God can fill a heart, that heart must first be washed. This cleansing is not only the physical act of baptism but the inner washing of the soul by God's truth, that is, God's Word.

It echoes the prophetic promise in Ezekiel, where God said:

> *"I will sprinkle clean water on you, and you shall be clean...*
> *I will give you a new heart and put a new spirit within you."*
> *(Ezekiel 36:25–26)*

To be born of water means to allow God to wash away the stains of sin and prepare the vessel for new life. It is repentance that opens the heart for renewal.

Born of the Spirit

But cleansing alone is not enough. There must be life—and that life comes only through the Holy Spirit.

To be "born of the Spirit" is to receive a divine infusion of God's own life and nature within. It is not simply turning over a new leaf or trying harder to do better. It is becoming a new creation, as Apostle Paul wrote:

"If anyone is in Christ, he is a new creation;
old things have passed away; behold, all things have become new."
(2 Corinthians 5:17)

The Spirit gives birth to spirit. What is born of the flesh—our natural nature—remains limited, fallen, and self-driven. But what is born of the Spirit carries heaven's DNA. It breathes the breath of God. It desires holiness, truth, and intimacy with the Father.

When a person is truly born of the Spirit, everything changes. Old appetites lose their grip. The mind begins to think differently. The heart beats with new passion for the things of God. The invisible becomes more real than the visible, and life itself takes on a new purpose.

Being born again is not a one-moment experience—it is a process, an intentional journey of transformation. It unfolds one change after another, one renewal after the next. The moment we accept the Lord Jesus Christ and believe in His finished work in our hearts, the process begins.

That first step—believing—opens the door for God to begin His divine work within us. From there, He starts stripping away the layers of the flesh, healing the broken places, and reshaping our desires. It is a continuous yielding, where we allow the **Spirit of God** to overtake our human nature until Christ is fully formed in us.

True rebirth is not just a confession—it is a lifelong surrender that allows the Holy Spirit to rewrite our nature with His own

The Wind That Moves Freely

Jesus likened the work of the Spirit to the wind— unseen, yet undeniable.

*"The wind blows where it wishes, and you hear the sound of it,
but cannot tell where it comes from and where it goes.
So is everyone who is born of the Spirit."*
(John 3:8)

You cannot see the wind, yet you can feel its touch and witness its power—trees bending, dust swirling, leaves dancing. In the same way, when the Spirit breathes upon a life, something unmistakable changes.

Old desires lose their hold.
Love for God awakens.
Peace floods the heart where fear once ruled.

No one can control or predict the Spirit's movement. He moves freely, with divine intention, breathing life into every heart that yields to Him. His work cannot be contained by human systems or limited by religious traditions. He comes like a rushing wind—quiet to some, fierce to others—but always bringing life.

Born Again — The Doorway Into the Kingdom

To be born again is not a symbolic phrase; it is a spiritual reality. It is the doorway into the Kingdom of God. Religion may reform the outer life, but only the Spirit can transform the inner man. Flesh gives birth to flesh, but the Spirit gives birth to spirit.

Until a person is born again, they may understand the *words* of God but never taste the *life* of them. But once the Spirit gives birth within, Scripture comes alive, prayer becomes conversation, and worship becomes communion.

This is the heart of true salvation—the moment when Heaven invades a human heart and eternity begins within.

CHAPTER 3

FOUNDATIONS OF SPIRITUAL WARFARE.

In the spiritual landscape, warfare is a reality that confronts us from the moment we enter this world. For many Africans, this reality is ingrained in our cultural and religious practices, shaping our perception of spirituality from an early age. However, as we delve deeper into the dynamics of spiritual warfare, a crucial issue emerges—one that challenges our understanding of our relationship with God.

The African church, renowned for its fervent prayers and spiritual warfare, often finds itself ensnared in a cycle where the focus on combating spiritual forces overshadows the importance of nurturing a personal relationship with God. While prayers for deliverance and victory are undeniably powerful, they should not overshadow the foundational aspect of our faith—communion with God.

Consider the scenario of receiving a call from a loved one, only to find that they spend the entire conversation engaged in conversation with someone else, leaving you feeling neglected and unheard. Similarly, when our prayers become solely focused on warfare, we risk overlooking the essential element of intimacy with God—the very foundation upon which our faith rests.

It's almost like picking up your phone to call God, but instead of speaking to Him, you start arguing with the devil while the Lord remains on hold. How, then, can you hear His voice—or give Him the chance to tell you which weapon to use in the very battle you're fighting?

The danger lies in equating our relationship with God solely to our ability to wage spiritual warfare. While spiritual battles are inevitable, they should not overshadow the primary purpose of our faith—to know and love God intimately. We must remember that our identity as children of God is rooted in Him, not in our ability to engage in warfare.

Furthermore, the prevalence of a prosperity-driven gospel has led many to seek God solely for material blessings, equating His love with worldly success. Yet, true intimacy with God transcends materialism, rooted instead in a deep understanding of His unconditional love for us.

Who shall separate us from the love of Christ? Shall tribulation, or distress, or persecution, or famine, or nakedness, or peril, or sword? As it is written:
"For Your sake we are killed all day long;
We are accounted as sheep for the slaughter."
Yet in all these things we are more than conquerors through Him who loved us. For I am persuaded that neither death nor life, nor angels nor principalities nor powers, nor things present nor things to come, nor height nor depth, nor any other created thing, shall be able to separate us from the love of God which is in Christ Jesus our Lord. The Apostle Paul's words in Romans offer a profound

perspective on God's love—a love that remains steadfast even in the face of adversity. It's a love so profound that nothing in this world can separate us from it, a love that transcends our circumstances and defines our identity as His beloved children.
- *Romans 8:35-39 NKJV*

The Apostle Paul's words in Romans offer a profound perspective on God's love—a love that remains steadfast even in the face of adversity. It's a love so profound that nothing in this world can separate us from it, a love that transcends our circumstances and defines our identity as His beloved children.

To address the foundational issue within the African church, we must recalibrate our focus, placing intimacy with God at the forefront of our spiritual journey. Just as a house cannot stand without a solid foundation, our faith cannot flourish without a deep, personal relationship with God.

Building this foundation requires intentional effort, prioritizing time in the quiet and secret place where we can commune with God. It's here that He reveals His heart to us, as the scriptures says- "But God has revealed *them* (the secrets) to us through His Spirit. For the Spirit searches all things, yes, the deep things of God.(1 Corinthians 2:11,) imparting wisdom and strategies for navigating the spiritual battlefield.

In this sacred space of intimacy, we discover the keys to effective spiritual warfare—strategies tailor-made for the specific battles we face. Whether through prayer, fasting, praise, or other spiritual disciplines, God equips us with the tools we need to overcome every obstacle.

As we realign our focus and deepen our intimacy with God, we position ourselves to experience His power and provision in ways we never thought possible. Our spiritual battles are no longer fought from a place of fear or desperation but from a position of strength and confidence in our identity as children of the Most High.

Therefore, let us prioritise intimacy with God above all else, knowing that from this foundation, every aspect of our spiritual lives will be strengthened and empowered. As we seek His face in the secret place, He will reveal Himself to us in ways that surpass our wildest imaginations, transforming us into mighty warriors for His kingdom.

Inquiring of the Lord Before the Battle

David was a mighty warrior—fearless, strategic, and anointed for victory. He fought Goliath when no one else dared to, conquered nations, and expanded the territory of Israel. Yet, in all his strength and triumphs, Scripture says something remarkable about him:

"...the Lord has sought out a man after His own heart..."
— *1 Samuel 13:14 (NKJV)*

David's greatness was not rooted merely in his skill as a warrior, but in his relationship with God. He was a man of deep communion—one who would not make a move, even in the heat of war, without first inquiring of the Lord. That was the true secret of his victories.

He understood something we often forget: spending time with God to seek direction is never a waste of time. It is the most strategic weapon in any battle.

The Danger of Acting Out of Emotion

When David returned to Ziklag and discovered that the Amalekites had invaded the city, burned it with fire, and taken captive all the women and children—including his own family—his men were ready to stone him out of grief and anger (*1 Samuel 30:1–6*).

In that moment, every human instinct would say, *"Act now! Go after them!"* But David didn't. Instead, the Bible says:

"So David inquired of the Lord, saying, 'Shall I pursue this troop? Shall I overtake them?' And He answered him, 'Pursue, for you shall surely overtake them and without fail recover all.'"
— *1 Samuel 30:8 (NKJV)*

David didn't let his emotions lead him—he let the Spirit of God lead him. And because he waited for

God's direction, he not only recovered everything but also gained more than he had lost.

This teaches us a vital truth: emotion-led action often leads to regret, but Spirit-led action leads to recovery and victory, and this is what often happens when people are mostly focused only on warfare without relationship with God. They tend to lose a lot and encounter what many warfare ministers call "collateral damage," which should never be the case if God is given His position first.

The Power of Inquiring Before Acting

Throughout Scripture, those who paused to seek the Lord before taking action always saw divine results. Inquiring of the Lord isn't hesitation—it's holy strategy, it is intimacy. It shifts the battle from your hands into God's hands.

When we stop to seek His counsel, He releases direction, timing, and divine alignment. Let's look at how this principle played out in the lives of Jehoshaphat, Joshua, and Moses—three leaders who discovered that victory begins not with movement, but with enquiry.

Jehoshaphat: Victory Through Worship and Waiting

(2 Chronicles 20)

When King Jehoshaphat heard that three great armies—Moab, Ammon, and Mount Seir—were marching against Judah, fear naturally filled his heart. But rather than rally his army, the Bible says:

"Jehoshaphat feared, and set himself to seek the Lord, and proclaimed a fast throughout all Judah."
— *2 Chronicles 20:3 (NKJV)*

He gathered the entire nation, from the youngest to the oldest, to seek the Lord together. They didn't plan a counterattack—they prayed. They didn't prepare swords—they lifted their voices in worship.

Jehoshaphat's prayer ended with these humble words:

"We have no power against this great multitude that is coming against us; nor do we know what to do, but our eyes are upon You."
— *2 Chronicles 20:12 (NKJV)*

That moment of surrender invited divine strategy. The Spirit of the Lord came upon Jahaziel, who prophesied:

"Do not be afraid nor dismayed because of this great multitude, for the battle is not yours, but God's."
— 2 Chronicles 20:15 (NKJV)

Jehoshaphat obeyed. The next morning, he appointed singers to go ahead of the army, praising God. As they worshipped, the Lord Himself set ambushes against their enemies. The three invading nations turned on each other until not one survived.

Jehoshaphat's inquiry produced strategy, and his obedience produced supernatural victory.

Joshua: The Painful Lesson of Acting Without Enquiry

(Joshua 7–8)

After the miraculous fall of Jericho, Joshua and Israel were confident. God had given them a mighty victory —but in their confidence, they made a costly mistake.

When they approached the next city, Ai, Joshua did not inquire of the Lord. He relied on past success and human assessment.

"Let not all the people go up... for they are few."
— Joshua 7:3 (NKJV)

But when the army went out, they were defeated. Thirty-six men died, and the people's hearts melted in fear. Joshua fell before the Lord, crying out in confusion. It was then that God revealed the hidden sin in the camp—Achan's disobedience. This revelation came by relationship.

The defeat had not come because Ai was strong, but because Joshua had moved without consulting God.

When Joshua repented and inquired of the Lord again, God gave him a new strategy:

"*Do not be afraid... take all the people of war with you, and arise, go up to Ai... lay an ambush for the city behind it."*
— Joshua 8:1–2 (NKJV)

This time, Joshua followed the Lord's plan—and the city of Ai fell completely.

Moses: Deliverance Through Divine Direction

(Exodus 14)

When the Israelites stood trapped between the Red Sea and Pharaoh's army, panic erupted. The people cried out in fear, accusing Moses of leading them to die in the wilderness.

But Moses did not react—he waited for God's command. And the Lord said:

"Why do you cry to Me? Tell the children of Israel to go forward. But lift up your rod, and stretch out your hand over the sea and divide it."
— *Exodus 14:15–16 (NKJV)*

In that divine moment, the impossible became possible. As Moses obeyed, the sea parted and Israel walked through on dry ground. The same waters that opened for them later swallowed their enemies.

If Moses had panicked and run, Israel would have perished. But because he paused to listen, he walked into a miracle.

Why Enquiring Brings Progress

When we inquire of the Lord, we move from:

- Reaction to revelation

- Emotion to direction

- Self-reliance to divine reliance

Every enquiry births clarity. Every pause births strategy. Every surrender invites heaven's intervention.

David, Jehoshaphat, Joshua, and Moses each faced impossible battles—but the difference between loss and victory was the moment they stopped to ask.

In our own lives, this truth remains:
Before every decision, before every confrontation, before every step forward—ask first. God never delays instruction; He perfects timing.

Lord, What Should I Pray Today?
Have you paused before prayer to inquire of the Lord what you should pray for? Have you experienced the transformative power of praying according to His leading, even when you don't fully understand the details?

I vividly recall the first time I embraced this strategy of seeking the Lord's guidance before praying. It was a revelation that astonished me, yet it profoundly impacted my prayer life. When I asked the Lord what I should pray about, He directed me to intercede for someone whose name I didn't recognize. Though I didn't know the person or their situation, I prayed fervently, trusting that God's purposes would be fulfilled in that person's life.

Indeed, prayer doesn't always require our full understanding of the circumstances. The Lord entrusts us with prayers for situations and individuals we may not comprehend because He knows the power of our intercession. As we yield to His leading, He unveils mysteries and entrusts us with divine insights into the lives of others. Intercession is actually a big part of our Christian walk that stems our of our personal relationship with God as He reveals deep secrets so that we may pray His will to pass on earth as it is in heaven. However, the topic of intercession is one for another book, as it goes deeper on its own.

This privilege of intimate communion with God extends beyond mere prophecy. It's about being attuned to His voice in the quiet moments of our secret place, where He reveals hidden truths and invites us to partner with Him in intercession. As His sons and daughters, we are entrusted with the sacred task of standing in the gap for others, even when we don't fully grasp the significance of our prayers.

Consider the night in May 2015 when the Lord interrupted my plans and revealed His own. Despite my initial doubts, His voice was clear, guiding me to surrender my desires and trust in His divine plan. Little did I know that His directive to return to South Africa from Texas would lead to a profound reunion with my siblings after many years of separation.

In hindsight, I marvel at the intricacies of God's plan and the depth of His love that orchestrated our family reconciliation. Though the journey was marked by uncertainty and wrestling, His faithfulness remained unwavering, guiding me every step of the way.

This experience serves as a testament to the intimacy God desires to share with each of us. He longs for us to seek His guidance, to trust in His wisdom, and to surrender our plans at His feet. For it's in the quiet moments of communion with Him that He imparts divine revelations and prepares us for the journey ahead.

So, as you reflect on your own prayer life, I encourage you to embrace the practice of seeking the Lord's guidance before you pray. Allow Him to lead you in intercession, trusting that He will unveil mysteries, impart wisdom, and guide you into deeper intimacy with Him.

May this revelation stir within you a hunger for the secret place, where you can commune with your Heavenly Father and receive divine insights that will transform your prayer life. And may you find joy and fulfilment in partnering with God to fulfill His purposes on earth.

CHAPTER 4

BUSY SERVING

In the hustle and bustle of ministry, and of life, it's easy to become consumed with serving the Lord while neglecting the most crucial aspect of our relationship with Him: intimate fellowship. The story of Martha and Mary serves as a poignant reminder of this truth.

Now it happened as they went that He entered a certain village; and a certain woman named Martha welcomed Him into her house. And she had a sister called Mary, who also sat at Jesus' feet and heard His word. But Martha was distracted with much serving, and she approached Him and said, "Lord, do You not care that my sister has left me to serve alone? Therefore tell her to help me." And Jesus

answered and said to her, "Martha, Martha, you are worried and troubled about many things. But one thing is needed, and Mary has chosen that good part, which will not be taken away from her.
-Luke10:38-42 NKJV

Martha, eager to ensure everything was in order for Jesus and His disciples, found herself distracted with much serving. In her earnest desire to attend to their needs, she became frustrated with her sister Mary, who chose to sit at the feet of Jesus, soaking in His presence and teachings. Martha's plea to Jesus reflects her overwhelmed state, seeking validation for her busyness and urging Mary to join her in her tasks.

However, Jesus gently rebuked Martha, recognizing her anxiety and preoccupation with many things. He highlighted the importance of prioritizing One thing above all else: intimate communion with Him.

Mary, who chose to sit at His feet and receive from Him, was commended for her decision, as it reflected a heart devoted to cultivating intimacy with the Lord.

In today's context, many individuals in ministry find themselves ensnared by the deceptive allure of busyness. While their intentions may be noble, the danger lies in prioritizing service over intimacy with God. The Creator of Life desires not only our service but also our presence—our willingness to sit at His feet and commune with Him.

The misconception that serving God replaces the need for personal fellowship with Him is a subtle lie propagated by the enemy. However, the truth remains: we are sons and daughters of God first and foremost, called to abide in His presence and draw from His wellspring of love and wisdom.

As ministers, whether we serve on the worship team, as ushers, pastors, media personnel, or in any capacity within the church, our service should flow from a heart intimately acquainted with the Father. Our message to the world should be rooted in the love of God, which we have personally experienced through our relationship with Him.

It's crucial to recognize that our service unto the Lord is an act of worship—a reflection of our reverence and adoration for Him. When we serve, whether in the church or elsewhere, our aim should be to point people to God, not to ourselves. We must guard against disseminating second-hand information or operating solely on borrowed knowledge, as it can lead to spiritual contamination and harm.

By 'second-hand information' I mean the habit of passing on information from the plethora of messages and sermons that are available to us from everyone and everywhere. We have a responsibility to test every spirit and test the context of every message preached to us, so that we can find a balance and walk in the truth of the scriptures.

Just as a brand ambassador represents a company's values and products, we represent the kingdom of God. Our words and actions should reflect the life and power of the Spirit, imparting truth and nourishment to those we encounter. Therefore, it's essential to prioritize personal communion with

God, allowing His Spirit to breathe life into our service and ministry.

In conclusion, we need to relinquish the mindset of being mere servants and embrace our identity as sons and daughters of the Most High God. May our service be a fragrant offering unto the Lord, borne out of the overflow of intimacy and communion with Him. As we sit at His feet and receive from Him, may we be empowered to serve others with humility, wisdom, and love.

Waiting on the Lord

The Bible tells us in Isaiah 40:31 (NKJV):
> *"But those who wait on the Lord*
> *Shall renew their strength;*
> *They shall mount up with wings like eagles,*
> *They shall run and not be weary,*
> *They shall walk and not faint."*

Even serving God requires strength.
To stay aligned with His will and remain faithful to the assignment He has given us takes strength. To grow

spiritually takes strength. Yet, the Scripture above reveals that the secret to receiving this strength lies in one word — waiting.

However, the word wait does not mean doing nothing. It means remaining in His presence — in stillness, in quietness, and in confidence — knowing that time spent with God is never wasted and never despised by Him.

Waiting is a spiritual discipline. It requires intentional stillness of heart in the secret place, where our souls cease from striving and our minds stop wandering, allowing the Lord — our Maker and our Husband — to speak, to instruct, and to strengthen us for the journey ahead.

This stillness doesn't happen by accident. It comes through intentional practice. As much as we may want to move forward with life, we must continually choose to be still before the Lord — to listen, to commune, and to be renewed in His presence. For in His presence, there is fullness of joy, and that joy overflows into strength — strength to walk, to endure, and to remain steadfast.

There are times when life feels heavy — when challenges make us forget that our strength is not our own. But we must remember that no one can reach their God-given finish line without consistently drawing strength from Him through the practice of waiting.

Over time, many believers grow restless and begin to seek words everywhere — from prophet to prophet, sermon to sermon, podcast to podcast. While spiritual teachings are valuable, God never intended for us to rely solely on secondhand revelation. We are not meant to live as if He speaks only through intermediaries. Through Christ Jesus, we have all been adopted as His children — invited into a personal, intimate relationship with HimTherefore, waiting becomes the sacred space where God deals with us individually — as though we were the only ones who matter to Him on earth. It is in that place that He begins to pour His life into ours. His life becomes our light, and that light becomes the life of men (John 1:4).

When the weight of life tries to drain us, the life of Christ within begins to flow again — like fountains of living water springing from our innermost being. This is what happens when we learn to wait: God reveals His depths, shares His secrets, and fills us daily with His strength and His Spirit.

CHAPTER 5

WHO DO MEN SAY I AM?

When Jesus came into the region of Caesarea Philippi, He asked His disciples, saying, "Who do men say that I, the Son of Man, am?" So they said, "Some say John the Baptist, some Elijah, and others Jeremiah or one of the prophets." He said to them, "But who do you say that I am?" Simon Peter answered and said, "You are the Christ, the Son of the living God." Jesus answered and said to him, "Blessed are you, Simon Bar-Jonah, for flesh and blood has not revealed this to you, but My Father who is in heaven. And I also say to you that you are Peter, and on this rock I will build My church, and the gates of Hades shall not [g]prevail against it. And

I will give you the keys of the kingdom of heaven, and whatever you bind on earth [h]will be bound in heaven, and whatever you loose on earth will be loosed in heaven."Then He commanded His disciples that they should tell no one that He was Jesus the Christ.
-Matthew 16:13-20 NKJV

In the profound exchange between Jesus and His disciples at Caesarea Philippi, He poses a pivotal question: "Who do you say that I am?" This question transcends mere theological discourse; it delves into the heart of personal revelation and identity.

Peter's response, "You are the Christ, the Son of the living God," reverberates through the ages, encapsulating the essence of true discipleship. Jesus's affirmation of Peter's confession highlights the transformative power of divine revelation— Peter's newfound understanding of Jesus's identity led to the revelation of his own identity.

In essence, knowing Jesus intimately leads to the discovery of our true selves. As Peter grasped the reality of Jesus's divinity, he was also unveiled to himself as a foundational pillar upon which the Church would be built. This divine exchange underscores the intimate connection between our identity in Christ and our purpose in His kingdom.

The servant mentality, rooted in a lack of understanding of one's identity, diminishes the fullness of our relationship with God. Jesus's revelation to Peter serves as a potent reminder that our primary identity is found in Him, not in the shifting opinions or labels of the world.

The concept of sonship in Christ transcends gender distinctions, encompassing all believers who are united with Him in spirit. It is a dynamic process of becoming, requiring continual communion with the Father and alignment with His will.

Scriptures affirm our identity as sons and daughters of God, chosen, beloved, and redeemed through Christ. Our sonship grants us access to the inheritance of the kingdom, empowering us to live lives of holiness and righteousness.

The process of becoming a son involves God's active involvement in our lives, pruning us for greater fruitfulness and conformity to His image. As we embrace our identity in Christ, we are liberated from the bondage of sin and empowered to live victoriously.

Our identity in Christ shapes our perspective, priorities, and pursuits. It positions us as ambassadors of His kingdom, called to proclaim His praises and reflect His light in a darkened world.

Ultimately, our highest calling is to be Christ-like, embodying His love, grace, and truth in all that we do. As we abide in Him and allow His Spirit to work in us, we manifest the glory of God and fulfill our purpose as His beloved children.

May we continually seek to deepen our understanding of our identity in Christ, allowing His truth to permeate every aspect of our lives. Let us embrace our sonship with humility and gratitude, walking in the fullness of His grace and the power of His Spirit.

It has almost become a spiritual pandemic in our generation — many believers live far below the quality of life that Jesus came to give. The root of this problem lies in one thing: we do not truly know or understand our identity in Him.

Jesus said,

> "I have come that they may have life, and that they may have it more abundantly."
> — John 10:10 (NKJV)

Yet many live defeated, fearful, or uncertain because they do not recognize who they are in Christ. Scripture reminds us that even a prince who does not know he is a prince will live as a slave:

> "I have seen servants on horses, while princes walk on the ground like servants."
> — Ecclesiastes 10:7 (NKJV)

We were created to reign as kings and priests on the earth — backed by the Spirit of God who dwells within us.

> "And has made us kings and priests to our God; and we shall reign on the earth."
> — Revelation 5:10 (NKJV)

When we forget our divine identity, we begin to live as victims of circumstances instead of victors through Christ. We become targets of the enemy instead of being the ones he fears. In truth, when we walk in our God-given authority, many of the things we now run from would begin to run from us.

> "Submit to God. Resist the devil and he will flee from you."
> — James 4:7 (NKJV)

Unfortunately, many believers today seem to apologize for who they are in Christ. In a world filled with many voices, religions, and philosophies, we often shrink back instead of standing boldly as ambassadors of Heaven.

> "Now then, we are ambassadors for Christ, as though God were pleading through us."
> — 2 Corinthians 5:20 (NKJV)

But we were never called to be timid or apologetic. The Word says,

> "For God has not given us a spirit of fear, but of power and of love and of a sound mind."
> — 2 Timothy 1:7 (NKJV)

When we come to truly know who we are in Christ, everything changes. The same transformation happened in the life of Peter. Once fearful and uncertain, Peter denied Jesus three times (Matthew 26:69–75). But after encountering the risen Christ and being filled with the Holy Spirit, he became a pillar of boldness.

> Jesus had earlier declared to him,
>
> "You are Peter, and on this rock I will build My church, and the gates of Hades shall not prevail against it."

— Matthew 16:18 (NKJV)

Later, in the book of Acts, we see that same Peter — once timid — now fearless, preaching Christ publicly and refusing to bow to threats:

> "But Peter and John answered and said to them, 'Whether it is right in the sight of God to listen to you more than to God, you judge. For we cannot but speak the things which we have seen and heard.'"
> — Acts 4:19–20 (NKJV)

What changed Peter? Revelation and relationship.
He spent time with Jesus. He beheld His glory. And as Scripture tells us,

> "But we all, with unveiled face, beholding as in a mirror the glory of the Lord, are being transformed into the same image from glory to glory."
> — 2 Corinthians 3:18 (NKJV)

The more we behold Him, the more we become like Him. The more we look to Jesus — in prayer, in the Word, in worship — the more His nature, boldness, and authority are formed within us.

When we walk in that identity, we no longer apologize for being who we are in Christ. We stop shrinking back and begin to manifest the glory of God within us. We remember that:

> "Greater is He who is in you than he who is in the world."
> — 1 John 4:4 (NKJV)

And that awareness changes everything.

CHAPTER 6

WHY DIDNT YOU COME TODAY?

In the simple yet profound moments shared with my late mother, I discovered a powerful truth about the nature of love and intimacy—a truth that transcends human relationships and extends to our relationship with God Himself.

Just as my mother cherished my presence in her office whenever I would be away from her for long, the Holy Spirit yearns for our presence in His presence. Sometimes, He simply desires us to be with Him, to share in the silence and stillness of His embrace. In those moments, love is communicated not through words or actions, but through the intimacy of shared presence.

Our busy lives often deceive us into believing that time spent in God's presence is time wasted. However, the opposite is true. In the stillness of His presence, profound transformation occurs.
Ministries are birthed, breakthroughs are realized, and lives are forever changed.

Just as my mother would inquire if I hadn't visited her office, the Holy Spirit beckons us to His presence, eagerly awaiting our arrival. He is a faithful timekeeper, always ready to commune with us in the cool of the day, just as He did with Adam in the garden of Eden.

Creating intentional time for intimacy with God is essential. This dedicated time, free from distractions and interruptions, honors our relationship with Him and fosters deeper intimacy. It is a sacred appointment, one that should be honored and cherished.

As we draw near to God in intimacy, He reveals Himself to us in gentle, loving ways. He delights in us as His beloved children, embracing us with His unfailing love and grace. In His arms, we find rest, strength, and security.

Maintaining a childlike posture before God is not a sign of weakness but of true greatness. Jesus Himself, though Son of God, exemplified humility and obedience, becoming the author of eternal salvation through His submission to the Father.

Therefore, let us embrace our identity as beloved children of God, basking in His love and presence. In His arms, we find our truest selves and discover the path to greatness—a path marked by humility, obedience, and unwavering devotion.

So, the next time the Holy Spirit whispers, "Why didn't you come today?" may we respond with a heart eager to commune with our Heavenly Father, knowing that in His presence, we find all that we need and more.

The Lord's Desire for Time with Us

The Lord delights in spending time with His children. His desire for fellowship is so personal that if you were to ask Him, "Lord, what time would You like to meet with me?" — He would answer. It may not be through an audible voice, but through a gentle prompting in your spirit.

Scripture shows us that even Jesus had a set time of fellowship with the Father.

> "Now in the morning, having risen a long while before daylight, He went out and departed to a solitary place; and there He prayed."
> — Mark 1:35 (NKJV)

It was Jesus' custom to rise before the sun and commune with God. I used to wonder, "What was Jesus praying about? He already knew the Father perfectly. He already knew His mission." Yet, Jesus still prioritized time alone with the Father.

Jesus' dependence on the Father was not because of ignorance but because of intimacy. Though He was fully divine, He modeled to us what it means to live as a human fully yielded to God. He desired constant fellowship — not for information, but for connection, renewal, and empowerment.

Throughout His ministry, Jesus was always spiritually aware. He knew the thoughts of men (John 2:24–25), discerned their intentions (Luke 5:22), healed the sick, raised the dead, cleansed lepers, and answered the hardest questions of His critics — not merely from human knowledge, but through the wisdom and whispers of the Holy Spirit within Him (John 5:19–20).

Everything Jesus did was to teach us how to live as restored sons and daughters of God on earth. That divine sensitivity — the ability to hear, see, and move with Heaven's direction — was what humanity lost when Adam and Eve fell.

At the beginning, the enemy didn't just tempt Adam and Eve to eat the fruit; he stole their identity by deceiving them into believing they were less than who God made them to be. Jesus said of the devil:

> "He was a murderer from the beginning… and the father of lies."

— John 8:44 (NKJV)

The "murder" began with the killing of man's divine identity — the loss of authority and spiritual awareness. But Jesus, the second Adam, came to restore that identity and authority (Romans 5:17). He showed us that through fellowship with the Father, we regain strength, wisdom, and dominion.

Even after long days of ministry, when He was tired and surrounded by crowds, Jesus withdrew to pray.

> "And when He had sent the multitudes away, He went up on the mountain by Himself to pray. Now when evening came, He was alone there."
> — Matthew 14:23 (NKJV)

This is the power of the secret place. Even when the body is weary, the Spirit of God can quicken and refresh you.

> "But if the Spirit of Him who raised Jesus from the dead dwells in you, He who raised Christ

from the dead will also give life to your mortal bodies through His Spirit who dwells in you."
— Romans 8:11 (NKJV)

God knows that our human strength will fail, but He also knows that His strength never does. That is why time in His presence is not a burden — it's a renewal. So, tiredness can never be a true excuse. Whether you are weary from work, ministry, parenting, or the demands of life — the Lord simply calls you to come as you are. The secret place is not for the perfect; it is for the willing.

When you come, He gives you strength —
- Physical strength to continue your daily tasks,
- Spiritual strength to overcome temptation,
- Emotional strength to stand in peace,
- Mental strength to carry wisdom, and even financial and relational strength through divine alignment.

The secret place is where exchange happens — your weakness for His power, your weariness for His presence, your emptiness for His fullness.

"Those who wait on the Lord shall renew their strength;
They shall mount up with wings like eagles,
They shall run and not be weary,
They shall walk and not faint."
— *Isaiah 40:31 (NKJV*

CHAPTER 7

THE FIRST TIME I HEARD HIM

Whenever someone asks me how it happened for me, I can't help but smile at the goodness of God. I always feel the same excitement that I felt on that exact day. Oh, even now I cannot believe this really happened to me, and has been happening ever since. I always stand in awe that God would speak to me. Me, who was lost and confused? Me, who was messed up and filthy, and yet He found me worthy to be embraced by Him.

We tend to drift away from the idea of spending time with God when our sin seems to be speaking louder than His truth. His truth is that "though our sins are like scarlet, they shall be white as snow. Though they are like crimson, they shall be like wool" (Isaiah 1:18 NKJV).

When you ask Him to forgive you, He forgives for real. When you ask Him to save you from a lifestyle of sin, that's why Jesus died on the cross at Calvary. When He died, He rose again on the third day. He didn't rise from the grave for you to always drown in sin's guilty stains. The resurrection of Jesus Christ from the dead means you also rose with Him, so if you fall, don't stay on the ground, for you are seated with Him in heavenly places. I am saying all that so you may know that the love of God won't disqualify you; you disqualify yourself, and you shouldn't. I will also say, the availability of grace towards us is to empower us to not be the embodiment of sin and therefore, you can live a sin-free life-by the grace of God which helps us in a time of need.

Do you honestly think that God didn't know that Adam and Eve had eaten the fruit when He went looking for them? I believe that our All-Knowing God knew exactly what had just happened, but He still went to Adam to show him that He was still willing to listen to him. The Bible shows us that after Adam pointed out to God that he was naked, the Lord still showed them love by making garments of skin for both Adam and his wife, Eve, and He clothed them (Genesis 3:21). What manner of love is that? A love so deep that even when we were the ones who were wrong, the Lord still opened Himself up and used His creative abilities to clothe us because there was a statement spoken that "I am naked." It seemed that being naked was the reason why Adam had hidden away from God at that moment, so the Lord dressed Him up. Maybe if Adam was clothed, then he wouldn't shy away from the Lord.

Do you know that the tree of knowledge of good and evil was not for God to eat, but for Adam? It is evident that the Lord knew already the difference between good and evil, but for Him to have uncontaminated fellowship with mankind, the fruit had to remain untouched. This was not for the Lord's sake, but for our sake.

Now the knowledge of evil is the reason why we continually feel unworthy of the work of God or the presence of God, but I am here to let you know that there is no place in scripture where He says you should come after you are clean. He says that you should come as you are, and He will clean you up. He wants you to go to Him naked, as you are, and He will clothe you. From a place of shame to a place of belonging. From a place of undeserving to Him finding you worthy. The love of God is wonderful in all its ways. All you have to do is receive it.

One night, I went to sleep wondering whether I should wake up earlier for my quiet time with Jesus because I knew my apartment would be noisy after a certain time, so I could only get up in the early morning or sleep late at night just to spend time with Him. While I was thinking about it, an 'idea' came to mind that I had to wake up at exactly 4 am, and so I went along with that 'idea.' I woke up feeling very excited and hoping that this time I would hear the Lord speak. I studied the word and I wrote some things down that were being highlighted to me in the word, and then I noticed that the message to me was that I had to go on a time of fasting. When I picked up the instruction, I felt really sad because I had been battling with fasting already. I had gone around asking people how to fast and no one had really told me what was supposed to be done or the way to do it right, but I remembered that God was my only help at that moment, so I decided to ask Him directly. I told Him that I understood everything that He had been trying to tell me, but I was already struggling with fasting already and that I would do it if He would find a way to teach me how to do it right.

The idea that many people have is that when the Lord speaks, there is lightning, storm, and thunder. They expect the very loud, strong, and powerful voice of God. So, when it doesn't happen that way, people seem to feel discouraged, or they don't believe that God has spoken indeed. I asked the Lord my question and a few moments later, while I sat waiting on Him, I saw within my heart what seemed like a chalkboard, and on this board were letters being written. The letters were I S A I A H 5 8, then the board disappeared. So, I wondered what that was about, but I quickly opened my bible to that scripture, only to realize that the title for that chapter is "Fasting that pleases God," in the New King James Version of the Bible. I could not believe it. I was so surprised, so I read through that chapter, line upon line, and it suddenly seemed as though my eyes were open to understanding this whole concept of fasting through that scripture. The Lord truly surprised me because I had always expected that strong and mighty, loud voice of God, but His ways are not my ways and His thoughts are not my thoughts.

Isaiah 58 made fasting so simple for me to understand. I understood that it is not just about denying myself food but that it is about sharing with others what I have. I understood that it is about being sensitive to the Holy Spirit, who will guide me as to what to do when I fast. I didn't need to go looking for answers outside anymore, for now, I had an understanding of what the Lord wanted from me. He just wanted me to obey Him, to spend time with Him, and to be sensitive to the Holy Spirit, for He would teach me all things.

I understood that fasting was a time when God wanted to be the only one in my heart. I understood that fasting was about breaking the bondages of wickedness. I understood that fasting was about being delivered from the oppression of the devil. I understood that fasting was about feeding the hungry, clothing the naked, and taking in the homeless. I understood that fasting was about being a light to others, so they can also find their way in Him. I understood that fasting was about giving what I have to others, and the Lord would reward me openly. I understood that fasting was about giving, for I too had been given. I understood that fasting was about being a healer to the brokenhearted. I understood that fasting was about being a peacemaker. I understood that fasting was about letting the Lord's light shine in my life. I understood that fasting was about bringing glory to His name. I understood that fasting was about me and the Lord. I understood that fasting was about loving one another. I understood that fasting was about bringing the kingdom of God on earth as it is in heaven.

I could go on and on about fasting, but the point is, do not be afraid to ask the Lord directly because He is always willing to teach you. He is willing to show you great and mighty things which you do not know. He is willing to guide you through whatever you are going through, and you will be a better person because of it.

Ways God Speaks To Us
There are many ways in which the Lord speaks to us, as inscribed in scripture, so we must always be alert to any of these ways. As I began to pay more attention, I concluded that there are quite a number of ways that He uses to speak to me, but I truly believe that those are not all the ways.

As mentioned earlier, the first one was two modes of communication, combined. One is Scripture, and the other is Vision.

Scripture:
Everything we need and every question we may have has its answer in the Word of God. I truly believe that if we wait and listen, every situation we

may encounter in life can be found in the Word of God, as well as solutions to every problem we face.

Let me use a few examples to illustrate this.

Are you in debt? The bible shows us in 2 Kings 4:1-7 that there was a woman who had a debt that her husband had left for her and she was about to lose her sons. Usually, people drowning in debt are about to lose something, whether it be a car, or a house or something very valuable to them.

A certain woman of the wives of the sons of the prophets cried out to Elisha, saying, "Your servant my husband is dead, and you know that your servant feared the Lord. And the creditor is coming to take my two sons to be his slaves."So Elisha said to her, "What shall I do for you? Tell me, what do you have in the house?" And she said, "Your maidservant has nothing in the house but a jar of oil."Then he said, "Go, borrow vessels from everywhere, from all your neighbors—empty vessels; do not gather just a few. And when you have come in, you shall shut the door behind you and your sons; then pour it into all those vessels, and set aside the full ones." So she went from him and shut the door behind her and her sons, who brought the vessels to her; and she poured it out. Now it came to pass, when the vessels were full, that she said to her son, "Bring me another vessel." And he said to her, "There is not another vessel." So the oil ceased. Then she came and told the man of God. And he said, "Go, sell the oil and pay your debt; and you and your sons live on the rest."

2 Kings 4:1-7 NKJV

We see that according to this scripture, we are never without anything. The Lord reminds us to use whatever may be in our hands to create wealth and pay off all debts. With His divine assistance, He then makes the increase. So, we cannot and should not be stuck in debt. But you wouldn't know this if you were not spending time with God because the Spirit behind the Word is His Spirit, and that Spirit leads us through His Word when we spend more time in it. The bible is filled with scriptures on how to know God, to know His ways, and how to navigate through life.

The Lord then uses the Word to communicate to us whatever He sees fit for us to do.

Another example of this topic would be the story of Ruth. In scripture, we find that there is hope for the woman who would have lost her husband. It is a story of restoration and it shows the Lord can restore. If you are in a season of grieving, as a widower, and the Lord places this story in your spirit, then you would be rest assured that He is working behind the scenes in your favor. If you are having issues with your siblings, there is the story of Jacob and Esau where the Lord helped in bringing peace between the brothers. Whenever you are in the situation of constant sickness in the house, the Word tells us to lay hands on the sick and they will recover. There are other stories of people who were sick, even to the point of death, but the Lord healed them. These situations shared in the Bible are real stories, of real people who went through real things and the Lord showed up for them. So, when He brings it to your remembrance, it becomes your ultimate responsibility to sit at His feet and figure out exactly what the Lord is saying to you. These things happen by constant fellowship with Him because it is not always the same problems that are solved by similar solutions. For example, we find a story in 2 Kings 3, that tells us that three nations were going to war with one nation, but they didn't have the victory, so they sought a prophet of God and He told them to dig ditches. The bible says the Kings of Israel, Judah, and Edom then dug the ditches and their livestock had water to drink, however; those ditches became like blood in the eyes of the Moabites and so the Moabites gave themselves into the hands of Israel, Judah, and Edom, for defeat. They did not have to fight or take over the way they knew how. All they had to do was dig ditches and those ditches were the means to their victory. But we find in the same Bible in 2 Chronicles 20, that the King of Judah – Jehoshaphat, was going to war with the Moabites once again and with the Ammonites, however; this time they did not have to dig ditches to become victorious. They went on a fast and then had to praise, and praising the Lord was their victory. In the same manner, not one solution works for every problem. We can only know these by divine inspiration from the Holy Spirit. We have to become very intentional in being still in His presence so that we can always be on par with the required strategies for that season, or for that battle. Time with God is never wasted, every moment becomes a moment of learning and a time of being equipped for this world. Do not take it lightly, do not take it for granted.

God speaks through music:
This might be a little confusing for those who have never heard about it. But I can safely say, this is my personal favorite way of God speaking to me. This is when random songs drop into your spirit. You might not have even heard that song in ages, but it comes back and rings in your spirit. This usually happens with Worship/Christian music. The Lord will project His message through that, and so it is important that we sing and listen to it while we sing, for the message. I have observed that when I am being warned to pray about a death in the family or being prepared for death, I start hearing songs of death drop in my spirit. When that happens, then I know it's something I should focus on in prayer. I have been warned about heartbreak coming my way through a song. I would find myself singing old

heartbreak songs that I used to listen to way-back-when. I even remember one time I met a guy and I thought I had fallen in love, and before I could even figure out what was happening, the Lord had begun telling me about the heartbreak I was falling into, through a particular song about having a heart attack, and oh did I not go through that heart attack for real? That is all on the negative side, but the Lord speaks through music on a positive scale too. There were times when a surprise would be coming and all of a sudden, a song would drop in my spirit and I would hear it all day long and I would think it was just in my head until the surprise arrives and I realize that the Lord had been speaking to me through that song, preparing me for the surprise. We must always stay in tune with the Lord because He is forever speaking. Let us not forget that.

Have you had a moment where you are in a situation that you have no idea if you will survive or how you will survive that season? While sitting and pondering upon the situation, you suddenly hear "
What the enemy
Meant for evil
God has turned it around

Turned it around
What the enemy
Meant for evil
God has turned it around
For my good
(Pastor Nathaniel Bassey)

Or maybe you are in a warfare season and then you just start hearing "There is power in the name of Jesus, to break every chain, break every chain."

I have learnt that in those situations, you have to turn on that song and play it, meditate on it until it becomes your reality. Things will change, and that's God responding to your situation.

God speaks through dreams:
I am going to be very honest. This once became my least favorite way of communication from the Lord. I began to dislike this method of communication when I found out that most times when I had a question or I was trying to enquire of the Lord for something, I found that it was very difficult to receive dreams concerning that thing, or that I would begin to dream

about sheep and goats - nothing to do with what I was searching for in the realms of God. There were times when the Lord gave me dreams, and they'd come to pass as it was shown in the dream.

I remember there was one particular dream where I was going through a heartbreak and the Lord revealed to me that it would happen and who the person was, and so I took it to prayer and told the Lord to have His way with it. I was not ready for that relationship to come to an end, but the Lord had already warned me about it in my dream. I remember this dream very well, because I was walking on a long road, with potholes on both sides of the road, and I was holding hands with this guy who was leading the way. Every time he would pass a pothole, he would lift my hand and tell me to jump. I would jump every time he says, and so we continued walking on that road until we came across a very huge pothole. It was huge enough that we would have had to jump off the road entirely to avoid it. But when he saw the huge pothole, he just jumped by himself and left me behind to fend for myself. When I jumped, I got swallowed by that pothole and I woke up from my dream. When I prayed about it, I was told by the Lord that the potholes in the dream represented the challenges in our relationship, and that the fact that he left me to fend for myself represented him leaving me to face the challenges of our relationship alone. I was told that if I didn't take charge and address the issues myself, then I would get swallowed up by those issues and they would destroy me. So, I did exactly that. I took charge of my relationship and tried to address every issue that arose, and so when the time came for us to part ways, I was fully ready to let go. I would also get dreams of death and usually they are warning dreams for me to pray about a certain situation or to be prepared for a certain situation. This is not to say that every dream from the Lord is a warning. The Lord also gives dreams to His children to prepare them for good things to come or just to reveal to us what we need to pray about or to give us direction. There are different types of dreams, and the Lord reveals to us what we need to know. We must always ask for clarity when we receive dreams from the Lord because without clarity, we could be misled and misinterpret His message.

God speaks through Preachers:
It is important that we stay connected to the Body of Christ so that we do not miss out on what the Lord is saying. A lot of times the Lord uses preachers to speak to us. I have experienced this countless times. There would be times when I am faced with a particular situation and I would hear the preacher talk about that particular thing that I am going through and it would feel as though the preacher is talking directly to me. It is important that we do not take this for granted. We should always be careful to pay attention to everything that is said during a service, for the Lord could be speaking directly to us.

God speaks through silence:
There are times when the Lord might not say anything at all. This usually happens when He has given us a Word about a certain situation and we have done nothing about it. He might remain silent until we do something about it. This is not to say that He is not speaking to us, but He is waiting on us to do something about the last Word He gave us. If we fail to do something about it, then He will remain silent until we do something about it. We see an

example of this in 1 Kings 22, when Ahab wanted to go to battle, he went to all the prophets of Baal, and they all told him to go to battle, but Jehoshaphat wanted to inquire of the Lord. So, Ahab called for Micaiah, and Micaiah told him to not go to battle, but Ahab didn't listen, he went to battle, and we see that Ahab died in that battle, just as Micaiah had prophesied. The Lord speaks, but it is our responsibility to listen and to obey immediately He says.

So, the Lord uses the sound of thin silence to speak to us. This is communication from within, not something heard with physical ears, but with spiritual ears. I, for one, have struggled with believing it was indeed the Lord speaking whenever I heard the still small voice. But I now understand what I didn't before: it takes consistency in listening. Quietness is a skill that can only be obtained through practice, a discipline that must be adhered to. While you are still learning His voice, you have to trust what you hear and measure it against the Word of God. Always remember, God never contradicts Himself. If you sense a contradiction, it's likely due to your own misunderstanding, as it's never truly one word against another.

Here are some ways to test the voice of God:

- You can test the voice of God through the peace that accompanies it. Philippians 4:7 tells us, "the peace of God which surpasses all understanding, will guard your hearts and minds through Jesus Christ."
- The voice of God can be tested by consistent relationship with Him.
- The voice of God can be tested by the truth it speaks. God is not a deceiver.
- You can test the voice of God by the freedom it brings, even if it leads to discomfort.
- The voice of God is right (Psalm 33:4).
- The voice of God is pure and brings sanctification.

There are many other ways to discern whether what or who you are hearing is indeed God. According to John 10:27, Jesus tells us that His sheep know His voice, and He knows them, and they follow Him. You begin to know Him by obeying the smaller instructions He gives. As He trusts you with bigger things, you'll see Him speaking more and in greater depth. But He speaks to everyone. All you have to do is listen. He is waiting for you, even now, to find that place in your heart and time in your schedule to commune with Him. The Holy Spirit yearns to commune with you. You are His number one priority, and it would honor Him greatly if you would honor Him by making time for Him.

Let Us Pray Right Here:

Heavenly Father, I ask now in the name of Jesus Christ that the dearly beloved one reading this with a heart really ready to encounter and relate with You in a new and fresh way, Lord, I pray that You would begin to show them Your most consistent form of communication. I ask, Lord, that You would sanctify them by Your Word so their ear gates may be pure and ready for You. Do a fresh thing in their life, Lord, I ask in Jesus' name. Amen!

CHAPTER 8

TO KNOW HIM IS TO HAVE ETERNAL LIFE.

> "And this is eternal life, that they may know You, the only true God, and Jesus Christ whom You have sent."
> (John 17:3)

Many people assume "eternal life" means simply living forever in Heaven. But Jesus defines it differently — not by duration, but by relationship. Eternal life begins the moment we come to truly know God through Christ.

Everyone — both saved and unsaved — will exist forever in spirit. But only those united with God through Jesus Christ will experience eternal life. The rest experience eternal separation, which is spiritual death (Romans 6:23).

So, in this context:
Eternal life = the restored relationship and intimate union between God and His people through Jesus Christ.

Eternal life doesn't start after death — it starts when you believe in Jesus.

"He who believes in the Son has everlasting life."
— *John 3:36*

Notice the word has — not will have. That means eternal life is a present possession for every believer.

It's the very life of God — His Spirit, His power, His nature — imparted to us at the moment of salvation (John 1:12–13; 1 John 5:11–12). When Jesus prayed John 17, He was revealing that eternal life isn't a future reward; it's a living relationship that begins now and continues forever.

The Greek word for know is ginōskō — meaning to know personally, intimately, and experientially. It's the same word used when Scripture says, "Adam knew Eve his wife" (Genesis 4:1).

So, when Jesus said eternal life is to know God, He meant that the essence of salvation is intimacy and union — a deep, living fellowship with the Father through the Son, empowered by the Holy Spirit.

This knowing is not academic — it's relational. It means:

- Knowing God's heart, not just His works.

- Hearing His voice, not just hearing about Him.

- Walking with Him daily, not visiting Him occasionally.

This is the restoration of Eden — humanity walking again with God in continual communion.

At creation, Adam and Eve walked with God in the cool of the day (Genesis 3:8). That was eternal life on earth — continual fellowship with the Source of life.

When sin entered, that relationship was broken, and humanity became separated from God.

When Jesus came, His mission was to restore that fellowship.

"I am the way, the truth, and the life. No one comes to the Father except through Me."
— John 14:6

Through His sacrifice, the barrier of sin was removed, making it possible for us to once again know God personally — not just as a distant deity, but as Abba Father (Romans 8:15).

The Greek word for "life" is zoē — the divine, God-kind of life. It's not biological (bios) life, but spiritual vitality — the very essence of God Himself.

"God has given us eternal life, and this life is in His Son. He who has the Son has life."
— 1 John 5:11–12

Eternal life, therefore, is Christ living in you. It's not only life after death — it's the life of Heaven flowing through you now. Everything connected to Him breathes life, while everything apart from Him decays and dies.

That's why believers who walk closely with God radiate peace, wisdom, and strength — they are drawing daily from the well of eternal life within (John 4:14).

Knowing God is not passive awareness — it's a transforming relationship. The more we know Him, the more we reflect Him.

"But we all, with unveiled face, beholding as in a mirror the glory of the Lord, are being transformed into the same image from glory to glory."
— *2 Corinthians 3:18*

When we spend time in His presence — in prayer, in the Word, in worship — we're changed. His character becomes our character, His heart becomes our heart, and His desires become ours.

That's why Apostle Paul said:

"That I may know Him and the power of His resurrection."
— Philippians 3:10

Even after encountering Jesus, Paul's greatest pursuit was still to know Him more. Eternal life deepens daily as we walk with Christ.

When Adam sinned, humanity lost fellowship — and with it, divine authority. Jesus, the second Adam, came to restore both.

By giving us His Spirit, He reconnected us to the Source of wisdom, strength, and dominion. That's why Jesus said:

"I have come that they may have life, and have it more abundantly."
— John 10:10

That "life" is zoē — divine, supernatural, eternal life. Through it, we reign in life (Romans 5:17).

Jesus didn't just say, "that they may know You," but also "and Jesus Christ whom You have sent."

This shows that eternal life flows only through knowing both the Father and the Son; acknowledging that Jesus is the full revelation of the Father's heart.

"He who has seen Me has seen the Father."
— John 14:9

To know Jesus is to know the Father. To reject Jesus is to reject the Father (1 John 2:23). There is no eternal life outside this relationship.

Eternal life is not something you wait to experience in Heaven — you can live it daily. Every time you commune with God, you taste eternity.

When you wake up and talk with Him, when you worship, when His peace fills your day — that's eternal life at work.

Heaven is not just a place — it's the presence of God. Eternal life is living in that presence here and now.

John 17:3 is not a theological statement — it's a divine invitation.
Jesus invites you into a lifelong relationship, not a religious routine.

God doesn't just want servants; He wants friends (John 15:15). He wants you to know His heart, not just His hand.

He invites you to walk with Him daily, talk with Him freely, and learn His ways intimately. This is the heartbeat of eternal life — union with the Father through the Son by the Spirit.

CHAPTER 9

BREAKING FREE FROM THE RELIGIOUS SPIRIT

What Is the Religious Spirit?

The religious spirit is a counterfeit of true spirituality — a demonic influence that imitates devotion to God while secretly opposing the Spirit of truth and the freedom found in Christ.

This spirit seeks to replace relationship with ritual, presence with performance, and humility with pride. It thrives in outward appearance, rules, and self-effort, yet resists the inner transformation that comes through the Holy Spirit.

Jesus often confronted this spirit in the Pharisees and scribes of His day:

> "This people honors Me with their lips,
> but their heart is far from Me;
> and in vain they worship Me,
> teaching as doctrines the commandments of men."
> — Matthew 15:8–9 (NKJV)

The religious spirit can exist anywhere — in churches, ministries, or even in sincere believers who began well but drifted into formality.
Its aim is to make us busy for God but disconnected from God.

The Nature and Work of the Religious Spirit

The religious spirit is subtle. It doesn't always look evil; it often appears moral, disciplined, and correct. But its fruit reveals its true nature.

Common Expressions:

1. Performance-Driven Faith — Trying to earn God's love through works instead of resting in His grace (Ephesians 2:8–9).
2. Judgment and Comparison — Measuring others' spirituality by appearances or traditions (Luke 18:9–14).
3. Pride in Knowledge or Position — Placing identity in ministry titles or intellect rather than in sonship (1 Corinthians 8:1).
4. Fear of Intimacy — Preferring structure over surrender.
5. Resistance to the Holy Spirit — Valuing control more than His flow (2 Corinthians 3:17).
6. Legalism and Condemnation — Emphasizing rules over grace, producing guilt rather than freedom (Romans 8:1–2).

The religious spirit cannot coexist with genuine intimacy, because intimacy grows only in humility and dependence, not in pride or self-righteousness.

How It Affects Our Relationship with God

When the religious spirit is active, it substitutes form for fellowship.

It causes believers to pray without connection, worship without encounter, and serve without joy.

Like the elder brother in the parable of the prodigal son (Luke 15:25–32), the religious believer may stay in the Father's house yet never enjoy the Father's heart.

Its Effects:
- Spiritual dryness: Prayer becomes mechanical and distant.
- Lack of revelation: Scripture becomes information, not transformation.
- Pride or inferiority: Either feeling spiritually superior or constantly unworthy.
- Inability to receive love: Believing God is pleased only by performance.
- Resistance to correction: Equating personal conviction with divine truth.

Ultimately, the religious spirit makes us servants instead of sons — working for God rather than walking with Him.

Jesus' Confrontation with the Religious Spirit

Throughout the Gospels, Jesus confronted this spirit head-on.
The Pharisees prayed, fasted, tithed, and studied Scripture — yet missed God standing right before them.

> *"You search the Scriptures, for in them you think you have eternal life; and these are they which testify of Me.*
> *But you are not willing to come to Me that you may have life."*
> *— John 5:39–40 (NKJV)*

The religious spirit blinds the heart to the living Christ. It honors tradition but ignores transformation — loves knowledge but despises encounter.
Jesus exposed it because it keeps people close to the things of God while far from the presence of God.

The Subtle Signs of a Religious Spirit

Below are some revealing attitudes and habits that expose the presence of a religious mindset.

1. Trying to Fix Everyone Else

If your prayer life revolves around others' faults rather than your own heart, you've stepped into deception.

> "Why do you look at the speck in your brother's eye, but do not consider the plank in your own eye?" — Matthew 7:3

The secret place is not a place of gossip but of transformation. When you stop trying to fix people, God begins to fix you.

2. Living Under Guilt and Shame

Religion tells you God only wants you when you're "clean."
But the Father's heart says, "Come as you are — I'll cleanse you."

> *"If we confess our sins, He is faithful and just to forgive..."* — 1 John 1:9

Guilt drives you away; grace draws you near.

3. Judging Who Deserves Redemption

If you ever think someone is "too far gone," remember: Jesus came for the lost.

> *"For the Son of Man has come to seek and to save that which was lost."* — Luke 19:10

Holiness restores — it doesn't reject.

4. Thinking You're Too Holy to Fall

Self-righteousness is spiritual pride in disguise.

> *"For He made Him who knew no sin to be sin for us, that we might become the righteousness of God in Him."* — 2 Corinthians 5:21

Righteousness bends low — it doesn't boast.

5. Craving Titles and Recognition

When your worth depends on applause, you've already lost sight of the cross.

> *"How can you believe, when you receive glory from one another..."* — John 5:44

True servants don't seek to be known — they seek to make Him known.

6. Always Learning, Yet Never Changing

Knowledge without transformation is religious vanity.

> *"Always learning and never able to come to the knowledge of the truth."* — 2 Timothy 3:7

The goal of revelation is relationship — not information.

7. Serving Out of Fear, Not Love

Fear says, "If I stop serving, God will replace me."

Love says, "I serve because I love Him."

> *"Perfect love casts out fear."* — *1 John 4:18*

God is not looking for terrified servants, but for sons and daughters who serve from love.

8. Refusing to Forgive

A heart that withholds mercy has forgotten how much mercy it received.

> *"Forgive us our debts, as we forgive our debtors."* — *Matthew 6:12*

Forgiveness releases both the offender and the offended.

9. Focusing on Outward Appearance

Religion polishes the outside; relationship cleanses the inside.

> "You clean the outside of the cup... but inside they are full of greed and self-indulgence." — Matthew 23:25 (NIV)

True holiness is measured by love, not by looks.

10. Rejecting Counsel and Correction

Even Jesus submitted to authority.

> "In the multitude of counselors there is safety." — Proverbs 11:14

Humility keeps the heart teachable and safe from deception.

The Way to Freedom

Freedom begins not by rebellion, but by returning to intimacy.
It's not about rejecting discipline but embracing grace.

a. Recognize and Repent

Admit where you've performed instead of loved, judged instead of served, or sought reputation over relationship.

> *"Now God commands all men everywhere to repent."* — Acts 17:30

Repentance is not punishment; it's liberation.

b. Return to First Love

> *"You have left your first love… repent and do the first works."* — Revelation 2:4–5

Fall in love with Jesus again — pray for delight, not duty. Worship for love, not approval.

c. Receive the Grace of Sonship

You are already accepted in Christ (Ephesians 1:6). Stop striving for what's already yours — the Father's love.

d. Pursue Presence, Not Performance

Create stillness for the Holy Spirit to refresh you.
Worship becomes encounter when the heart rests in Him.

e. Walk in the Spirit

> *"If we live in the Spirit, let us also walk in the Spirit." — Galatians 5:25*

> Depend on His leading daily, not on routines or formulas.

f. Stay Humble and Teachable

A surrendered heart is a protected heart.
Humility invites grace; pride repels it.

Fruits of Freedom

When the religious spirit is broken, your soul breathes again.

You begin to experience:
- Joy in His presence (Psalm 16:11)

- Revelation through the Word (2 Corinthians 3:16)
- Compassion over criticism (Matthew 9:36)
- Confidence in sonship (Romans 8:15–16)
  - Boldness in prayer (Hebrews 4:16)
  - Freedom in worship (John 4:23–24)

"Where the Spirit of the Lord is, there is liberty."
— 2 Corinthians 3:17

The Spirit of religion produces bondage — but the Spirit of sonship produces intimacy.

CHAPTER 10

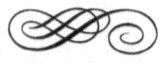

NO ONE SEES ME AND LIVES

> But," He said, "you cannot see My face; for no man shall see Me, and live."
> — Exodus 33:20 (NKJV)

Moses was not a casual seeker — he was a man who had already seen God's power, presence, and miracles. He had watched the Red Sea part, manna fall, and a nation delivered by God's mighty hand. Yet his heart longed for more.

He didn't just want to see what God could do — he wanted to know who God was.

So he cried out:

> "Please, show me Your glory." — Exodus 33:18

This was not the prayer of an immature believer but of an intimate friend of God — one who had tasted His presence and wanted to dwell in it permanently.

But God's answer carries both mercy and mystery:

> "You cannot see My face, for no man shall see Me and live."

At first, it may sound like a denial — but hidden within it is a divine invitation to transformation.

God's statement reveals the contrast between divine holiness and human frailty.
Sin corrupted the nature of man to the point where our physical and spiritual condition could not withstand the full radiance of God's glory.

To "see His face" means to behold the fullness of His unveiled nature — His purity, majesty, and consuming light.
The human body and unredeemed soul simply cannot survive that intensity.

It's not that God hides because He is cruel — He hides because His essence is too glorious for fallen flesh to endure. His holiness would consume corruption instantly.

> "For our God is a consuming fire." — Hebrews 12:29

The glory of God doesn't kill because it's evil — it kills because it's too good for what is still impure.

When God told Moses he couldn't see His face and live, He was actually protecting him.
This was divine mercy — not divine rejection.

Instead, God made a way for Moses to experience His presence safely:

> *"Here is a place by Me, and you shall stand on the rock. So it shall be, while My glory passes by, that I will put you in the cleft of the rock and will cover you with My hand while I pass by."* — *Exodus 33:21–22*

This is prophetic symbolism. The Rock represents Christ.

God was foreshadowing the day when humanity could once again behold His glory — but only through the covering of Christ.
Outside of Jesus, the glory kills; in Jesus, the glory transforms. Moses stood in the cleft of the Rock — we now stand in Christ.

When Jesus came, He became the visible expression of the invisible God (Colossians 1:15).
He clothed divinity in flesh so that humanity could once again encounter God and live.

> "And the Word became flesh and dwelt among us, and we beheld His glory..." — John 1:14

The very glory that once required God's protective hand now became flesh and walked among men — approachable, touchable, and full of grace and truth.
Through the cross, the separation between man and God was removed.
What Moses could only glimpse from behind the veil,

we now experience through the indwelling Holy Spirit.

Under the Old Covenant, seeing God's face meant death.
Under the New Covenant, seeing God's face means life.

The same glory that once consumed sin from the outside now transforms us from within.

> "But we all, with unveiled face, beholding as in a mirror the glory of the Lord, are being transformed into the same image from glory to glory…" — 2 Corinthians 3:18

When Moses came down from Mount Sinai, his face shone with reflected glory.
But when we come out of communion with Jesus, we radiate transformed glory.
We don't just carry reflected light — we carry indwelling light.
The veil that separated man from God's face has been torn (Matthew 27:51).

Through Christ, we are invited back into what Moses longed for — face-to-face communion.

To "see His face" now means to encounter the depth of His heart — His will, His love, His presence.
Every true believer is called to this intimacy.

In prayer, worship, and fellowship with the Holy Spirit, we begin to "see" the invisible. Not with natural eyes, but with the eyes of the spirit.

> *"Blessed are the pure in heart, for they shall see God."* — Matthew 5:8

This "seeing" changes us.
Each encounter purifies, softens, and realigns our hearts to reflect His likeness.

The greatest revelation of Exodus 33:20 is that what Moses could not see, we now can.

> *"For it is the God who commanded light to shine out of darkness, who has shone in our hearts to give the light of the knowledge of the*

glory of God in the face of Jesus Christ." — 2 Corinthians 4:6

The "face" that once meant death now shines as the face of Jesus — the perfect revelation of God's love and glory.
Through His Spirit, we can now behold God's face daily and live.

This is the highest form of intimacy — not just serving God, but beholding Him.

Exodus 33:20 once symbolized the distance between God and man, but in Christ, it now symbolizes the depth of restored relationship.

The more we behold His glory, the more our flesh dies — not in destruction, but in transformation.
Self fades, pride breaks, and we become like Him.

So yes — in the flesh, no man can see God and live.
But in the Spirit, no man can see God and remain the same.

Moses stood outside the promise we now live inside.
He saw God's back; we behold His face.
He hid in a rock; we are hidden in Christ.

To see His face is no longer forbidden — it's our inheritance.
To live after seeing Him is no longer impossible — it's our transformation.

The scripture in Exodus 33:20 states, "But He said, 'You cannot see My face; for no man shall see Me, and live." This passage seems straightforward, indicating that encountering God directly would result in death. However, when we delve deeper into the context and consider the experiences of individuals like Moses, we uncover a profound spiritual truth.

Moses, despite being told that seeing God's face would result in death, had a unique encounter. He communed with God face to face, and yet he lived to tell the tale. This apparent contradiction prompts us to explore the deeper meanings of encountering God.

When we approach the Bible with a surface-level understanding, we risk missing the deeper insights that the Holy Spirit reveals to us. Through the illumination of the Holy Spirit, we gain a clearer understanding of God's Word.

While it's true that encountering God's unfiltered glory would overwhelm mortal beings, there's a spiritual dimension to seeing God that transcends physical sight. When Moses communed with God face to face, it wasn't a mere physical encounter but a deep spiritual communion. His face shone with the radiance of God's presence, indicating a transformation at the spiritual level.

Similarly, when we enter into the presence of God, whether through prayer, worship, or meditation on His Word, we undergo a spiritual transformation. In His presence, our old selves begins to die, and we are reborn into His likeness. This process of spiritual renewal is ongoing and progressive.

The apostle Paul encourages believers not to conform to the standards of this world but to be transformed by the renewing of their minds (Romans 12:2). This transformation occurs as we encounter God in a personal and intimate way, and by allowing His Spirit to work within us.

I can attest to the transformative power of encountering God personally in my own life. When I first surrendered my life to Christ, I experienced a profound sense of confusion and uncertainty. However, through a series of encounters with the Lord, I began to experience His presence in a tangible way.

One significant encounter occurred when I found myself in a foreign land, feeling isolated and alone. In the depths of my despair, I encountered the presence of Jesus in a tangible way. Though I couldn't see Him with my physical eyes, I felt His presence surrounding me, offering comfort and companionship.

In that moment, Jesus revealed Himself to me as a friend who understood my deepest longings and fears. Though I had sought companionship from others, He showed me that He was the truest and most faithful friend I could ever have.

As I continued to walk with the Lord, He began to reveal areas of my life that needed to be surrendered to Him. One such area was my music choices, which were not in line with His standards. Though I initially resisted His prompting, I eventually obeyed His instruction to remove secular music from my life.

Through this obedience, I experienced a transformation in my thought patterns and speech. The music I listened to began to reflect the values and truths of God's Word, leading to a greater sense of spiritual sensitivity.

God's transformational work in my life didn't stop there. He continued to refine my character and conform me to His image, correcting my speech and attitudes along the way. Though the process was challenging at times, I experienced His patience and grace as He gently guided me toward holiness.

In reflecting on my journey of encountering God, I've come to understand that true transformation occurs when we surrender ourselves completely to Him. As we draw near to God in intimacy and relationship, we begin to reflect His character more fully.

Just as individuals throughout Scripture encountered God in unique ways and came to know Him by different names, so too can we experience the multifaceted nature of God's character as we seek Him earnestly. Whether as Provider, Comforter, or Friend, God reveals Himself to each of us in ways that resonate with our deepest needs and desires.

Ultimately, encountering God requires us to die to ourselves—to surrender our own agendas and desires in order to fully embrace His presence and purpose for our lives. As we yield to His transformative work within us, we begin to see glimpses of His glory reflected in our own lives, drawing us ever closer to the likeness of Christ.

CHAPTER 11

THE CALL TO INTIMACY

In the Gospel of John, we encounter a profound unveiling of Jesus' heart—His relentless desire for intimate communion with those who believe in Him. Every chapter of John echoes the same invitation: "Come closer. Abide in Me. Know Me."

In John 14, Jesus gives us one of the most tender glimpses into this divine longing:

> "In My Father's house are many mansions; if it were not so, I would have told you.
> I go to prepare a place for you. And if I go and prepare a place for you, I will come again and receive you to

Myself; that where I am, there you may be also."
— *John 14:2–3 (NKJV)*

As I meditated on these words, I was deeply moved by Jesus' yearning for us to be where He is. This is not merely a future promise of Heaven—it's an invitation into present intimacy. His heart burns for relationship, not routine; for fellowship, not formality.

Jesus is jealous for our undivided affection. He doesn't desire a relationship defined by distance or dependence on intermediaries. He wants you. Not your pastor's walk with Him, not your leader's revelation—yours. In a culture that often elevates personalities over Presence, Jesus' words remind us that no leader, no system, and no structure can replace personal fellowship with Him.

A true shepherd leads the flock to the Shepherd, not to themselves. And Jesus identifies Himself clearly:

"I am the way, the truth, and the life. No one comes to the Father except through Me."
— *John 14:6 (NKJV)*

Through Christ alone, we enter the heart of the Father. He is the living doorway into communion—the bridge that reconnects humanity to divine intimacy.

But Jesus did not stop there. Knowing that His physical departure would leave His disciples vulnerable, He introduced the greatest gift of companionship—the Holy Spirit.

> *"And I will pray the Father, and He will give you another Helper, that He may abide with you forever— the Spirit of truth, whom the world cannot receive, because it neither sees Him nor knows Him; but you know Him, for He dwells with you and will be in you."*
> — *John 14:16–17 (NKJV)*

This Helper is not distant. He abides. His role is to draw us into continual fellowship with Jesus, teaching us, reminding us of truth, and guiding us into obedience.

> *"But the Helper, the Holy Spirit, whom the Father will send in My name, He will teach you all things, and bring to your remembrance all things that I said to*

> *you."*
> *— John 14:26 (NKJV)*

The Holy Spirit is Heaven's answer to separation—our eternal Companion who keeps us connected to the presence of Jesus. Yet, our disobedience and distractions often clutter our spiritual hearing. The gentle whispers of God can be drowned out by the noise of our own desires. This is why Jesus emphasized abiding.

> *"Abide in Me, and I in you. As the branch cannot bear fruit of itself,*
> *unless it abides in the vine, neither can you, unless you abide in Me."*
> *— John 15:4 (NKJV)*

To abide means to dwell, to remain, to stay close. It's the essence of intimacy—the Secret Place within the heart where the Spirit and soul commune without interruption. Jesus promises that if we abide in Him and His words abide in us, we will live in the flow of answered prayer and divine fruitfulness.

> *"If you abide in Me, and My words abide in you, you will ask what you desire, and it shall be done for*

you."
— *John 15:7 (NKJV)*

This is not a transactional promise; it's relational. The more we dwell in Him, the more our desires align with His will. Intimacy produces obedience, and obedience invites greater revelation.

Jesus made this truth beautifully clear:

*"He who has My commandments and keeps them, it is he who loves Me.
And he who loves Me will be loved by My Father, and I will love him and manifest Myself to him."*
— *John 14:21 (NKJV)*

Obedience is the language of intimacy. To those who love and obey Him, Jesus promises manifestation—a personal unveiling of His presence. The reward for love is more of Him.

In John 17, we hear the deepest cry of Jesus' heart as He prays to the Father on our behalf:

*"Father, I desire that they also whom You gave Me may be with Me where I am,
that they may behold My glory which You have given*

Me; for You loved Me before the foundation of the world."

— John 17:24 (NKJV)

This is the ultimate expression of the Secret Place—the longing of Jesus for eternal fellowship with us, both now and forever. His desire is not merely to save us, but to dwell with us.

The Gospel of John reveals Jesus not only as Savior but as Lover, Friend, and Bridegroom of the soul. His invitation is simple yet profound: "Come and abide."

He has prepared a place for us—not only in eternity but in His presence here and now. He calls us to step beyond religion and return to relationship, to rediscover the sweetness of walking with Him daily in the secret chambers of the heart.

May we respond to His call with wholehearted devotion, abiding in His love until every part of us echoes His prayer in John 17:21:

"That they all may be one, as You, Father, are in Me, and I in You; that they also may be one in Us."

CHAPTER 12

THE HILL OF THE LORD

The Psalmist poses a profound question in Psalm 24:3-5: Who may ascend to the hill of the Lord? Who may stand in His holy place? The answer lies in the qualities of one's character: clean hands, a pure heart, avoidance of idolatry, and truthfulness in speech.

Hill of the Lord — The Path to Holy Access

> *"Who may ascend into the hill of the Lord?*
> *Or who may stand in His holy place?*
> *He who has clean hands and a pure heart,*
> *Who has not lifted up his soul to an idol,*
> *Nor sworn deceitfully."*

— *Psalm 24:3–4 (NKJV)*

The Cry for Access

Every true seeker of God eventually faces this question:

Who can really stand in His presence?

David's words are not for the curious but for the hungry. This question rises from a heart that longs to dwell where God dwells, not merely to visit. To "ascend the hill of the Lord" is to move beyond ordinary devotion into divine intimacy — to enter the realm where God reveals His secrets and trusts you with His presence.

Many believers worship at the foothills, satisfied with blessings, miracles, and answered prayers. But few choose the climb. The hill of the Lord represents elevation — not of status, but of consecration. Each step upward requires surrender, cleansing, and purity.

This hill is not physical — it is spiritual. It is the place where the self dies, and only the Spirit breathes.

Throughout Scripture, mountains symbolize encounters with God:
- Moses climbed Mount Sinai and received the Law (Exodus 19).
- Elijah ascended Mount Carmel and called down fire (1 Kings 18).
- Jesus was transfigured on a high mountain (Matthew 17).

In each case, the mountain represented a place of separation, revelation, and transformation. The higher they climbed, the more distractions fell away.

You cannot ascend the hill of the Lord and remain unchanged. The climb strips you of self-dependence, pride, and impurity. It reveals who you truly are when no one is watching.

Clean Hands — Purity of Action

Clean hands speak of what you do — your external actions, your dealings, your conduct. They represent righteousness expressed through daily life.

> *"Draw near to God and He will draw near to you. Cleanse your hands, you sinners; and purify your hearts, you double-minded."*
> — *James 4:8*

Having clean hands means refusing to manipulate, cheat, deceive, or compromise integrity for gain. It means your service to God and others comes from honesty, not hidden agendas.

Daniel's story gives us a glimpse of what clean hands look like. When he refused to eat the king's food or bow to idols—even at the risk of his life—his external conduct reflected an inner devotion to God. His actions were an overflow of his consecration.

Clean hands don't mean sinless perfection; they speak of a heart that is quick to repent and hands quick to make things right. It's the posture of one who walks in truth even when no one is watching.

In today's world, clean hands look like the business owner who refuses to bribe, trusting God as their source; the pastor who will not twist Scripture for gain; the believer who chooses truth over reputation; or the worshipper who sings for God's pleasure, not man's applause, or money.

When your actions reflect truth, your worship rises before God like holy incense.

A Pure Heart — The Purity of Motive

If clean hands describe your actions, then a pure heart defines your motives. It's not just about what you do, but why you do it.

Many people do the right things for the wrong reasons—to be seen, applauded, or validated. But God weighs the heart, not the appearance. "Man looks at the outward appearance, but the Lord looks at the heart." (1 Samuel 16:7)

A pure heart is undivided; it wants God more than it wants to look good before others. It serves not for recognition, but out of love. It gives without wanting praise, loves without expecting return, and obeys even when no one notices. A pure heart doesn't chase position—it chases presence.

Mary of Bethany's quiet act of worship captures this essence. When she poured out her expensive perfume on Jesus' feet (John 12), it wasn't for attention—it was pure devotion. Others misunderstood her, but Heaven understood her heart.

When our motives are purified by love, our intimacy deepens. The pure in heart see God because they want nothing more than Him.

Not Lifting the Soul to Idols — The Purity of Worship

"Who has not lifted up his soul to an idol…" — Psalm 24:4a

An idol is anything that competes with God for our affection or attention. It may not be a carved statue—it can be success, relationships, ministry, influence, reputation, or even spiritual gifts.

The danger of a religious generation is idolizing ministry over intimacy—loving the work of God more than the God of the work. When Israel made the golden calf (Exodus 32), they weren't rejecting God outright—they wanted to worship their own way. That's what idolatry is: creating a version of God we can control.

We do this subtly when we idolize leaders, chase platforms more than prayer, or make career and comfort higher priorities than obedience. When our emotions, trust, and identity are attached to anything other than God, our soul is lifted toward an idol.

You cannot climb high while your heart clings low. True worship is exclusive affection. It is surrender that says, "Jesus, You alone."

Nor Sworn Deceitfully — The Integrity of Spirit

The presence of God demands truth in the inward parts. "Behold, You desire truth in the inward parts." — Psalm 51:6

Integrity is the language of the hill of the Lord. It is impossible to walk closely with God while living a double life. To "swear deceitfully" means to make promises you don't intend to keep, to project holiness outwardly while hiding compromise inwardly.

God calls us to transparency—to a life where our words and our worship agree. To say "God told me" when it's our own will speaking, or to maintain a public image that doesn't match our private life, is to wear a mask before the Holy One.

Those who climb the hill of the Lord have learned that truth attracts glory. They no longer hide—they confess, and in confession, they are purified for communion.

The Reward of Ascending

"He shall receive blessing from the Lord, and righteousness from the God of his salvation." — Psalm 24:5

The reward for clean hands and a pure heart is not applause—it's access. God gives such people revelation, authority, and closeness others only dream of. They become carriers of His presence, walking sanctuaries of His glory in boardrooms, churches, and homes.

You cannot buy that favor; it is birthed in purity. The ones who live near the fire of His presence become flames themselves.

The Generation That Seeks His Face

"This is Jacob, the generation of those who seek Him, who seek Your face." — Psalm 24:6

This is the prophetic generation God is raising—seekers of His face, not His hand. They crave the hill, not the hype. They want presence, not platform. Their hands are clean, their hearts pure, their souls undistracted.

These are the ones who will host the glory of God in homes, nations, and movements, because they've allowed the fire of holiness to refine them. Their pursuit is not performance—it is presence.

The Ascent Is an Invitation

The hill of the Lord is not climbed once—it's ascended daily. Every sunrise comes with a whisper: "Come up higher."

You can't climb in pride; humility is your rope.

You can't climb while carrying idols; let go and ascend light.

You can't climb while hiding sin; confession clears your path.

The climb is continual because intimacy is alive. Every step upward is another surrender, another layer of flesh falling away until only love remains.

When your heart is purified, the hill becomes your home. The Secret Place is no longer a moment—it becomes a lifestyle.

If you find yourself struggling with consistency in your spiritual walk, it's crucial to examine your life honestly. Are there areas of sin that create distance between you and God? Sin disrupts our communion with a holy God and hinders our ability to ascend to His presence.

God is holy, and He desires holiness from His people. While His grace allows us to approach His throne, we cannot take advantage of His grace to continue living in sin. Repentance is not merely verbal confession but a tangible turning away from sinful practices and aligning our lives with God's standards.

Some areas that are highlighted in scripture, for repentance:

1. Fornication: Engaging in sexual activities outside the context of marriage defiles the temple of the Holy Spirit. Repentance involves submitting our sexuality to God's standards and waiting for the right season for intimacy within marriage.

2. Gossip: The destructive power of gossip is emphasized in scripture. Repentance entails refraining from spreading rumors or speaking ill of others, recognizing the harm it causes to relationships and souls.

3. Idolatry: Anything that takes precedence over God in our lives becomes an idol. Repentance involves prioritizing God above all else, seeking His will before our desires or pursuits.

4. Adultery: Infidelity in marriage not only violates the covenant between spouses but also dishonors God. Repentance requires fidelity to both God and one's spouse, acknowledging the sanctity of marriage.

5. Hatred: Whether directed towards oneself or others, hatred is incompatible with God's love. Repentance involves letting go of bitterness and embracing forgiveness and love, reflecting God's character.

6. Self-dependence and pride: Relying on oneself and exalting one's abilities above God's sovereignty leads to pride. Repentance entails surrendering control to God, acknowledging His lordship over our lives.

Scripture warns against living according to the desires of the flesh, listing behaviors such as adultery, fornication, hatred, jealousy, and selfish ambition as incompatible with the kingdom of God. The fruit of the Spirit, on the other hand, includes love, joy, peace, patience, kindness, goodness, faithfulness, gentleness, and self-control (Galatians 5:22-23).

As we yield to the Holy Spirit, abandoning the cravings of our self-life, we experience the transformative power of God's grace. Our lives become characterized by righteousness and holiness, enabling us to ascend to the hill of the Lord and dwell in His presence.

Repentance is not a one-time event but a continual posture of humility and surrender before God. It involves confessing our sins, receiving God's forgiveness, and actively turning away from sinful practices. Through repentance, we access the deeper realms of intimacy and fellowship with God, fulfilling the Psalmist's call to those with clean hands and pure hearts to ascend to the hill of the Lord.

Let's Pray

Father, I come before you humbly, acknowledging my need for your forgiveness and mercy. I recognize that I have fallen short of your glory and have sinned in the following areas:

- Pride: Lord, forgive me for the times I've exalted myself above others and relied on my own strength rather than depending on you.

- Impatience: I confess my tendency to become frustrated and anxious when things don't go according to my plans. Help me to trust in your timing and have patience in all circumstances.

- Neglecting prayer: Forgive me, Lord, for neglecting my prayer life and failing to seek you diligently. Help me to prioritize communion with you daily.

- Critical spirit: I repent of the times I've judged others harshly and spoken words of criticism. Teach me to show grace and compassion to those around me.

- Selfishness: Lord, forgive me for putting my own desires and interests above the needs of others.

Transform my heart to be more selfless and considerate.

- Lustful thoughts: I confess my struggle with impure thoughts and desires. Purify my mind and cleanse me from all unrighteousness.

- Fear: Forgive me, Lord, for allowing fear to dictate my actions and decisions. Help me to trust in your sovereignty and walk in faith.

I surrender all these areas of my life to you, Lord, and ask for your forgiveness and cleansing. Fill me afresh with your Holy Spirit and empower me to live a life that honors and glorifies you.

In Jesus' name, Amen.

CHAPTER 13

OBEDIENCE — GOD'S LOVE LANGUAGE

If you love me, you will obey my commandments

John 14:15

Love That Obeys

Many speak of loving God, yet few realize that in God's kingdom, love is proven not by emotion but by obedience. Heaven measures love not by how passionately we sing, cry, or speak about God — but by how quickly and faithfully we obey His voice.

Jesus didn't say, "If you love Me, sing to Me." He said, "If you love Me, keep My commandments."

Obedience is the tangible proof of love. It's how God reads our hearts. In His eyes, love without obedience is noise — but obedience born of love is worship.

Real intimacy with God will always be tested through obedience. You can't say you love Him deeply if you constantly resist His leading. True relationship with God will require you to lay down what you love most, to demonstrate that He truly sits on the throne of your heart.

The Nature of Divine Instruction

Hearing God isn't always a sweet exchange of tender words. Yes, there are moments when His presence feels gentle, healing, and comforting — but intimacy also brings weight. It comes with divine requests, uncomfortable truths, and instructions that stretch your faith.

When God speaks, He often interrupts comfort. He'll ask for the very thing you didn't want to part with — your Isaac, your security, your reputation, your resources — not because He wants to take from you, but because He wants to see if He truly has you.

When Abraham finally heard God call his name in Genesis 22, it wasn't to bless him immediately, but to test him:

Then He said, "Take now your son, your only son Isaac, whom you love, and go to the land of Moriah, and offer him there as a burnt offering on one of the mountains of which I shall tell you."This was not an emotional exchange; it was an invitation into deeper trust. God was saying, "You've walked with Me long enough to enjoy My blessings — now will you trust Me enough to surrender them?" -Genesis 22:2

Obedience, then, becomes the furnace of intimacy — where love is refined and proven genuine.

Intimacy as a Test of Surrender

Intimacy with God is beautiful — but it's also dangerous to your comfort zone. The closer you draw to Him, the more He will ask of you. He will use intimacy as a mirror, showing you the things still competing for your heart.

When God asks for something, it's not because He needs it; it's because it still has a hold on you.

He asked Abraham for Isaac, not because He desired human sacrifice, but because Isaac represented Abraham's promise, his joy, his legacy — the very thing he waited years for. God wanted to know if Abraham loved the gift more than the Giver.

He asked the rich young ruler to sell all he had and give to the poor (Matthew 19:21), not because He despised wealth, but because wealth had become the man's identity. His possessions owned him, though he thought he owned them.

He asked the disciples to leave their nets — their livelihood, their income, their safety — and follow Him (Matthew 4:19).

He asked Mary to surrender her reputation, carrying a child before marriage (Luke 1:38).

He asked Peter to step out of the boat — to do something that defied logic (Matthew 14:29).

Every act of intimacy brings a moment of testing. Every encounter births an instruction. Every instruction reveals who truly reigns in your heart.

The Language of Sacrifice

To walk with God is to live in the rhythm of surrender. God speaks obedience as His native language; love translates it into action.

When God asks for something material — money, houses, cars, opportunities, or even relationships — He is not trying to strip you of blessings but of attachments.

He doesn't want your possessions; He wants your permission.

Many believers say they desire to "hear God's voice," yet when He speaks, His requests feel unreasonable. He'll whisper, "Give that away," or "Let that person go," or "Move to a place you don't understand."

It is at that point that intimacy becomes a test. Will you still call Him good when obedience costs you something?

Obedience is not always convenient. Sometimes it's lonely. Sometimes it means walking by faith with tears in your eyes and no map in your hands. But every obedient step builds an altar — and on that altar, your heart learns to worship beyond comfort.

Modern-Day Isaacs

God still asks for Isaacs today.

He asks for the business you built with your strength, to see if you'd still trust Him without it.

He asks for your savings, to teach you that provision doesn't begin in your bank account but in His covenant.

He asks for your car, not to leave you stranded, but to reveal that your mobility comes from His favor, not your engine.

He asks for your time, your platform, your voice — not because He wants less for you, but because He wants to entrust you with more.

Each time you release something precious at His request, you make space for something greater — His presence, His plan, His glory.

Abraham never truly lost Isaac. The moment he proved obedience, God provided a ram — a symbol that when love obeys, provision follows.

Obedience Unlocks Revelation

Many want new revelation without new obedience. But revelation comes through response. God will not reveal more to someone who ignores what He already said.

In John 14:21, Jesus declared:

He who has My commandments and keeps them, it is he who loves Me. And he who loves Me will be loved by My Father, and I will love him and manifest Myself to him."

Notice — the manifestation of Jesus comes after obedience.

You don't see more of God until you obey what He last said.

When Abraham lifted the knife in obedience, God revealed Himself as Jehovah Jireh — The Lord Who Provides. Had Abraham disobeyed, that revelation would have remained hidden.

Every new level of obedience unveils a new dimension of God.

Love That Costs Something

The depth of love is revealed by the depth of sacrifice.

David understood this when he said:

"Then the king said to Araunah, "No, but I will surely buy it from you for a price; nor will I offer burnt offerings to the Lord my God with that which costs me nothing.

Love that costs nothing is love that means nothing.

When you obey God at a cost, Heaven takes notice. Angels move, atmospheres shift, and your heart expands in capacity to love Him more. Obedience keeps you empty of idols and full of God.

Obedience Is Worship

Worship is more than singing — it's surrender.

Every act of obedience is a song sung in Heaven's language. Every "yes" to God is a note of love that echoes in eternity.

When Abraham raised the knife, it wasn't a violent act; it was worship. God called it that:

And He said, "Do not lay your hand on the lad, or do anything to him; for now I know that you fear God, since you have not withheld your son, your only son, from Me."- Genesis 22:12

Obedience reveals reverence. It declares that your heart is His home, your possessions His tools, and your life His testimony.

The Reward of Obedience

Obedience never leaves you poorer — it only positions you for divine exchange. When Abraham obeyed, he didn't lose a son; he gained a revelation and a covenant. When Peter left his boat, he didn't lose his career; he gained a calling. When Mary surrendered her reputation, she birthed the Savior.

Obedience is the currency of intimacy.

You cannot buy God's love — but you can show it through obedience.

When you say yes to God in secret, Heaven responds in public.

Conclusion — Love That Listens, Faith That Follows

To love God is to obey Him. To know God is to trust Him. To walk with God is to surrender continually.

True intimacy will always bring you to a place of sacrifice — not to destroy you, but to refine you. God doesn't ask for what you love to take it away; He asks to prove that nothing stands between you and Him.

In the end, obedience is not about loss — it's about alignment. It's how Heaven recognizes who truly loves Him.

Because in God's language, "I love You" sounds like "Yes, Lord."

CHAPTER 14

THE COST OF THE SECRET PLACE

"Then said Jesus unto his disciples, If any man will come after Me, let him deny himself, and take up his cross, and follow Me."

— Matthew 16:24

The Hidden Price of Proximity

The closer you draw to God, the more you begin to realize — the secret place is not just about rest; it's about refinement. It's not only a place of comfort but a furnace of transformation.

Many desire the glory of God's presence but few are willing to endure the fire that purifies those who dwell there.

To know God deeply is to allow Him to strip away everything that competes for His place in your life. Intimacy with God is not cheap — it comes at the price of your will, your comfort, your ambitions, and often, your image before men.

When Moses asked, *"Show me Your glory,"* God's response wasn't casual (Exodus 33:18–23). Before Moses could behold even a glimpse of that glory, he had to be hidden in the cleft of the rock — a narrow, uncomfortable space — while God covered him with His hand.

That is the picture of the secret place: hidden, narrow, and protective, but also uncomfortable.

The higher you climb with God, the narrower the road becomes.

The Mountain Principle

Every person God used mightily had a "mountain." Moses had Mount Sinai, Elijah had Mount Carmel, and Jesus had the Mount of Olives — places of solitude, consecration, and testing.

The mountain represents separation — not to isolate you, but to insulate you from the noise of the world. It's the place where the crowd cannot go.

When Moses went up, the rest of Israel stayed below. They wanted God's acts, but Moses desired His ways (Psalm 103:7). Many settle for goosebumps and blessings, but few press beyond into the realm where God's heart is revealed.

Every ascent with God costs you something on the ground.

You cannot climb and cling at the same time.

The Weight of Glory

Paul wrote, *"For our light affliction, which is but for a moment, worketh for us a far more exceeding and eternal weight of glory" (2 Corinthians 4:17).*

The weight of God's glory rests only where the flesh has been crucified. The secret place will always expose what must die before God can trust you with more.

Before Jesus carried resurrection power, He first carried the cross.

Before Abraham saw the promise fulfilled, he had to offer Isaac.

Before Joseph wore the robe of rulership, he wore the garments of betrayal and prison. He wore the garment of faithfulness to God even in the midst of temptation.

Before David was crowned king, he was hidden in caves and pursued by Saul. He wore what seemed like weakness even when he could have killed Saul and carried on with life.

The greater the call, the deeper the crushing.

The higher the anointing, the more personal the breaking.

God hides His most powerful vessels in seasons of obscurity, pruning, and testing — not to punish them, but to purify their motives.

The Gethsemane Moment

Even Jesus, the Son of God, faced the cost of intimacy in Gethsemane. It was there that His will and the Father's will wrestled.

He prayed, "Father, if You are willing, take this cup from Me; yet not My will, but Yours be done" (Luke 22:42).

That is the heart of every secret place dweller — yielded will.

True intimacy is not just in worship; it's in surrender.

It's not in the multitude of words; it's in the posture that says, "Whatever You ask, Lord, even if it costs me, the answer is yes."

Gethsemane is where intimacy becomes obedience.

It's where the wine of purpose is pressed out of the grapes of submission.

The Pain of Separation

The deeper you walk with God, the fewer people will understand your path.

God will call you into seasons where you must walk alone — not because He's abandoned you, but because He's consecrating you.

When God began to speak to Abraham, He said, "Leave your country, your people, and your father's household, and go to the land I will show you" (Genesis 12:1).

Separation was the first step to revelation.

You cannot bring everyone into your secret place season. Some relationships are too loud for the quiet whisper of God's voice. Some habits, environments, and even ministries can no longer fit the dimension God is calling you into.

God prunes not to reduce you, but to prepare you.

Modern-Day Cost

The cost of intimacy in our time may not always look like deserts and mountains — it often looks like:

- Saying no to certain opportunities because they'll draw you out of alignment.

- Giving away money or possessions when God says to, even when it stretches your faith.

- Turning down platforms that elevate your name but silence your convictions.

- Walking in humility when you're misunderstood.

- Obeying God's instruction that makes no logical sense, but perfect spiritual sense.

Many believers want the oil but not the crushing that produces it. Yet the anointing you carry is only as deep as the altars you've built in secret.

The fragrance of a surrendered life cannot be faked; it comes only from the fire of personal sacrifice.

The Reward of the Hidden Life

Though costly, the secret place produces the greatest treasure — the presence of God Himself. It's in that hidden place that your heart is refined, your faith is strengthened, and your identity is solidified.

Moses came down from the mountain and his face shone (Exodus 34:29).

That's what the secret place does — it changes your countenance. When you've been with God, you no longer need to announce it. His glory announces you.

When others see you, they sense Him.

That's the true evidence of intimacy — transformation.

The secret place is not for the faint-hearted.

It is for those who are willing to be pruned, purified, and processed until only Christ remains.

The invitation into the secret place is the invitation into death — death to self, ego, ambition, and control — so that the life of Christ can flow freely through you.

The cost is high, but the reward is immeasurable: to know Him, and to be known by Him.

CHAPTER 15

THE SECRET PLACE RECLAIMED

"Draw near to God and He will draw near to you." —
James 4:8 NKJV

It wouldn't do any of us justice to speak about intimacy with God without exploring the practical journey of building it. As you begin, remember — this isn't about religion or rigid rules. It's about relationship.

God doesn't expect you to copy someone else's walk with Him. He relates to each of us personally, uniquely, and tenderly. The key is simply to start — to turn your heart toward Him, and He will meet you there.

James reminds us that when we take the first step to draw near to God, He moves toward us in response. You cannot wait passively, hoping He will come closer on His own — He already has.

When Jesus died, "the veil of the temple was torn in two from top to bottom" (Matthew 27:50–51 NKJV). That moment declared an open invitation for all of us to enter His Presence freely. Heaven's door was unlocked. The Holy of Holies was no longer distant. The Father was saying, "Come."

Now it's your turn to answer that invitation.

The Holy Spirit — The Person Who Waits to Walk With You

As we've shared before, the Holy Spirit is not an "it" — He is a Person. It's remarkable how easily people personify Satan, yet struggle to recognize the Holy Spirit as personal, relational, and alive.

If you desire true intimacy with God, you must learn to know the Holy Spirit. He is the third Person of the

Godhead, fully God — your Comforter, Helper, Advocate, and Friend.

To walk closely with Him, learn to host His presence. Treat Him like the most honored guest in your home. Speak to Him often. Welcome Him. Let Him know He is desired and cherished.

This isn't about ticking off spiritual checklists — it's about cultivating companionship with the very Spirit who raised Christ from the dead and now dwells in you.

The Holy Spirit loves to talk. He longs to teach, guide, correct, and comfort you. Start by acknowledging Him, then speak — and listen. You'll be surprised how gently yet clearly He responds.

Quiet Time With the Holy Spirit

Your relationship with God will grow as you give Him dedicated, intentional time. Quiet time is sacred; it's where intimacy is birthed and deepened.

Here's how to begin:

1. Set a meeting time: Schedule uninterrupted time with Him — even if it means waking up earlier. Your consistency communicates value.

2. Obey promptly: When He gives an instruction, respond quickly. Delayed obedience is still disobedience.

3. Create a sacred space: Designate a peaceful spot where you meet God — a place of stillness, free from noise, filled with your Bible, journal, and worship.

4. Enter with praise: Approach His presence with thanksgiving and joy. Gratitude ushers in His glory.

5. Let Him lead: Don't script your time. Flow with His presence. If He stirs you to sing, pray, or simply sit in silence — follow His lead.

6. Be authentic: Speak from your heart, not from rehearsed words. Use your own voice. God desires honesty more than eloquence.

7. Journal your journey: Write what you hear, feel, or sense in prayer. Over time, these pages will become your testimony of His faithfulness.

Above all, protect this time. Guard it fiercely from distractions. Your secret place is your altar — the meeting point between heaven and earth.

Returning to the Heart of Fellowship

By practicing these steps and surrendering to the leading of the Holy Spirit, you'll begin to notice something: God isn't distant. He's near — waiting for your awareness to awaken.

The more you prioritize His presence, the more you'll sense His nearness in everything — in your thoughts, your work, your rest, your breath.

This is the journey of intimacy: not a one-time encounter, but a lifelong communion.

So today, step back into the secret place.
Make room for Him.
Speak — and listen.

Worship — and wait.

Let the Holy Spirit lead you deeper into the knowledge of God's love.

Because at the end of it all, this is what it means to truly live:

To know Him, and to be known by Him.

Welcome home — back to your secret place.

About Author

Suzeey Tina is a passionate intercessor, writer, and teacher called to help believers rediscover the beauty of intimacy with God. Through her ministry, Fortified Zion, she empowers others to build deep personal fellowship with the Holy Spirit and live from the secret place with power, purity, and divine purpose. Her journey is marked by surrender, restoration, and a relentless pursuit of God's presence — themes that echo through her writings and teachings. Suzeey's desire is simple yet profound: to awaken hearts to know God personally, walk in His voice daily, and live as reflections of His love on earth.

suzeeytina@gmail.com

www.ingramcontent.com/pod-product-compliance
Lightning Source LLC
Chambersburg PA
CBHW031249290426
44109CB00012B/508